T3-BHM-108

Four Corners

Jack C. Richards · David Bohlke

3B

Student's Book

CAMBRIDGE
UNIVERSITY PRESS

CAMBRIDGE UNIVERSITY PRESS
Cambridge, New York, Melbourne, Madrid, Cape Town,
Singapore, São Paulo, Delhi, Mexico City

Cambridge University Press
32 Avenue of the Americas, New York, NY 10013-2473, USA

www.cambridge.org
Information on this title: www.cambridge.org/9780521127325

© Cambridge University Press 2012

This publication is in copyright. Subject to statutory exception
and to the provisions of relevant collective licensing agreements,
no reproduction of any part may take place without the written
permission of Cambridge University Press.

First published 2012
2nd printing 2013

Printed in Lima, Peru, by Empresa Editora El Comercio S.A.

A catalog record for this publication is available from the British Library.

ISBN 978-0-521-12727-1 Full Contact 3A with Self-study CD-ROM
ISBN 978-0-521-12732-5 Full Contact 3B with Self-study CD-ROM
ISBN 978-0-521-12747-9 Teacher's Edition 3 with Assessment Audio CD / CD-ROM
ISBN 978-0-521-12743-1 Class Audio CDs 3
ISBN 978-0-521-12712-7 Classware 3
ISBN 978-0-521-12740-0 DVD 3

For a full list of components, visit www.cambridge.org/fourcorners

Cambridge University Press has no responsibility for the persistence or
accuracy of URLs for external or third-party Internet Web sites referred to in
this publication, and does not guarantee that any content on such Web sites is,
or will remain, accurate or appropriate. Information regarding prices, travel
timetables, and other factual information given in this work are correct at
the time of first printing, but Cambridge University Press does not guarantee
the accuracy of such information thereafter.

Art direction, book design, photo research, and layout services: Adventure House, NYC
Audio production: CityVox, NYC
Video production: Steadman Productions

Authors' acknowledgments

Many people contributed to the development of *Four Corners*. The authors and publisher would like to particularly thank the following **reviewers**:

Nele Noe, **Academy for Educational Development, Qatar Independent Secondary School for Girls**, Doha, Qatar; Yuan-hsun Chuang, **Soo Chow University**, Taipei, Taiwan; Celso Frade and Sonia Maria Baccari de Godoy, **Associaçao Alumni**, São Paulo, Brazil; Pablo Stucchi, **Antonio Raimondi School** and **Instituto San Ignacio de Loyola**, Lima, Peru; Kari Miller, **Binational Center**, Quito, Ecuador; Alex K. Oliveira, **Boston University**, Boston, MA, USA; Elisabeth Blom, **Casa Thomas Jefferson**, Brasilia, Brazil; Henry Grant, **CCBEU – Campinas**, Campinas, Brazil; Maria do Rosário, **CCBEU – Franca**, Franca, Brazil; Ane Cibele Palma, **CCBEU Inter Americano**, Curitiba, Brazil; Elen Flavia Penques da Costa, **Centro de Cultura Idiomas – Taubate**, Taubate, Brazil; Inara Lúcia Castillo Couto, **CEL LEP – São Paulo**, São Paulo, Brazil; Geysa de Azevedo Moreira, **Centro Cultural Brasil Estados Unidos (CCBEU Belém)**, Belém, Brazil; Sonia Patricia Cardoso, **Centro de Idiomas Universidad Manuela Beltrán**, Barrio Cedritos, Colombia; Geraldine Itiago Losada, **Centro Universitario Grupo Sol (Musali)**, Mexico City, Mexico; Nick Hilmers, **DePaul University**, Chicago, IL, USA; Monica L. Montemayor Menchaca, **EDIMSA**, Metepec, Mexico; Angela Whitby, **Edu-Idiomas Language School**, Cholula, Puebla, Mexico; Mary Segovia, **El Monte Rosemead Adult School**, Rosemead, CA, USA; Dr. Deborah Aldred, **ELS Language Centers, Middle East Region**, Abu Dhabi, United Arab Emirates; Leslie Lott, **Embassy CES**, Ft. Lauderdale, FL, USA; M. Martha Lengeling, **Escuela de Idiomas**, Guanajuato, Mexico; Pablo Frias, **Escuela de Idiomas UNAPEC**, Santo Domingo, Dominican Republic; Tracy Vanderhoek, **ESL Language Center**, Toronto, Canada; Kris Vicca and Michael McCollister, **Feng Chia University**, Taichung, Taiwan; Flávia Patricia do Nascimento Martins, **First Idiomas**, Sorocaba, Brazil; Andrea Taylor, **Florida State University in Panama**, Panamá, Panama; Carlos Lizárraga González, **Groupo Educativo Angloamericano**, Mexico City, Mexico; Dr. Martin Endley, **Hanyang University**, Seoul, Korea; Mauro Luiz Pinheiro, **IBEU Ceará**, Ceará, Brazil; Ana Lúcia da Costa Maia de Almeida, **IBEU Copacabana**, Copacabana, Brazil; Ana Lucia Almeida, Elisa Borges, **IBEU Rio**, Rio de Janeiro, Brazil; Maristela Silva, **ICBEU Manaus**, Manaus, Brazil; Magaly Mendes Lemos, **ICBEU São José dos Campos**, São José dos Campos, Brazil; Augusto Pelligrini Filho, **ICBEU São Luis**, São Luis, Brazil; Leonardo Mercado, **ICPNA**, Lima, Peru; Lucia Rangel Lugo, **Instituto Tecnológico de San Luis Potosí**, San Luis Potosí, Mexico; Maria Guadalupe Hernández Lozada, **Instituto Tecnológico de Tlalnepantla**, Tlalnepantla de Baz, Mexico; Greg Jankunis, **International Education Service**, Tokyo, Japan; Karen Stewart, **International House Veracruz**, Veracruz, Mexico; George Truscott, **Kinki University**, Osaka, Japan; Bo-Kyung Lee, **Hankuk University of Foreign Studies**, Seoul, Korea; Andy Burki, **Korea University, International Foreign Language School**, Seoul, Korea; Jinseo Noh, **Kwangwoon University**, Seoul, Korea; Nadezhda Nazarenko, **Lone Star College**, Houston, TX, USA; Carolyn Ho, **Lone Star College-Cy-Fair**, Cypress, TX, USA; Alice Ya-fen Chou, **National Taiwan University of Science and Technology**, Taipei, Taiwan; Gregory Hadley, **Niigata University of International and Information Studies, Department of Information Culture**, Niigata-shi, Japan; Raymond Dreyer, **Northern Essex Community College**, Lawrence, MA, USA; Mary Keter Terzian Megale, **One Way Línguas-Suzano**, São Paulo, Brazil; Jason Moser, **Osaka Shoin Joshi University**, Kashiba-shi, Japan; Bonnie Cheeseman, **Pasadena Community College** and **UCLA American Language Center**, Los Angeles, CA, USA; Simon Banha, **Phil Young's English School**, Curitiba, Brazil; Oh Jun Il, **Pukyong National University**, Busan, Korea; Carmen Gehrke, **Quatrum English Schools**, Porto Alegre, Brazil; Atsuko K. Yamazaki, **Shibaura Institute of Technology**, Saitama, Japan; Wen hsiang Su, **Shi Chien University, Kaohsiung Campus**, Kaohsiung, Taiwan; Richmond Stroupe, **Soka University, World Language Center**, Hachioji, Tokyo, Japan; Lynne Kim, **Sun Moon University (Institute for Language Education)**, Cheon An City, Chung Nam, Korea; Hiroko Nishikage, **Taisho University**, Tokyo, Japan; Diaña Peña Munoz and Zaira Kuri, **The Anglo**, Mexico City, Mexico; Alistair Campbell, **Tokyo University of Technology**, Tokyo, Japan; Song-won Kim, **TTI (Teacher's Training Institute)**, Seoul, Korea; Nancy Alarcón, **UNAM FES Zaragoza Language Center**, Mexico City, Mexico; Laura Emilia Fierro López, **Universidad Autónoma de Baja California**, Mexicali, Mexico; María del Rocío Domínguez Gaona, **Universidad Autónoma de Baja California**, Tijuana, Mexico; Saul Santos Garcia, **Universidad Autónoma de Nayarit**, Nayarit, Mexico; Christian Meléndez, **Universidad Católica de El Salvador**, San Salvador, El Salvador; Irasema Mora Pablo, **Universidad de Guanajuato**, Guanajuato, Mexico; Alberto Peto, **Universidad de Oxaca**, Tehuantepec, Mexico; Carolina Rodriguez Beltan, **Universidad Manuela Beltrán, Centro Colombo Americano**, and **Universidad Jorge Tadeo Lozano**, Bogotá, Colombia; Nidia Milena Molina Rodriguez, **Universidad Manuela Beltrán** and **Universidad Militar Nueva Granada**, Bogotá, Colombia; Yolima Perez Arias, **Universidad Nacional de Colombia**, Bogota, Colombia; Héctor Vázquez García, **Universidad Nacional Autónoma de Mexico**, Mexico City, Mexico; Pilar Barrera, **Universidad Técnica de Ambato**, Ambato, Ecuador; Deborah Hulston, **University of Regina**, Regina, Canada; Rebecca J. Shelton, **Valparaiso University, Interlink Language Center**, Valparaiso, IN, USA; Tae Lee, **Yonsei University**, Seodaemun-gu, Seoul, Korea; Claudia Thereza Nascimento Mendes, **York Language Institute**, Rio de Janeiro, Brazil; Jamila Jenny Hakam, **ELT Consultant**, Muscat, Oman; Stephanie Smith, **ELT Consultant**, Austin, TX, USA.

The authors would also like to thank the Four Corners editorial, production, and new media teams, as well as the Cambridge University Press staff and advisors around the world for their contributions and tireless commitment to quality.

Scope and sequence

Functional language	Listening and Pronunciation	Reading and Writing	Speaking
Interactions: Giving an opinion Asking for agreement	**Listening:** Common proverbs A personality quiz **Pronunciation:** Reduction of *don't you*	**Reading:** "The Signs of the Zodiac" Descriptions **Writing:** My personality	• Interview about personality traits • *Keep talking:* Left-brain versus right-brain quiz • Discussion about personality assumptions • Information exchange about friends and their personalities • *Keep talking:* Interviews about special people and things • Guessing game to match people and their personality descriptions
Interactions: Giving an approximate answer Avoiding answering	**Listening:** A survey on grocery shopping habits Award winners for environmental work **Pronunciation:** Stress in compound nouns	**Reading:** "One-of-a-Kind Homes" An article **Writing:** A letter about an environmental issue	• Discussion about community environmental problems • *Keep talking:* "Green" quiz • Survey about water usage • Cause and effect • *Keep talking:* Possible outcomes in different situations • Solutions to environmental issues
Interactions: Apologizing Accepting an apology	**Listening:** Apologetic phone calls A radio call-in show **Pronunciation:** Sentence stress	**Reading:** "Addy's Advice" Emails **Writing:** A piece of advice	• Tips for healthy relationships • *Keep talking:* Advice for relationship problems • Role play to apologize and make excuses • Speculations about classmates • *Keep talking:* Speculations about people • Discussion about relationship problems
Interactions: Advising against something Considering advice	**Listening:** Three problems Interviews about accomplishments **Pronunciation:** Stress shifts	**Reading:** "A Walk Across Japan" An interview **Writing:** An accomplishment	• Interview about personal experiences • *Keep talking:* "Find someone who" activity about personal experiences • Role play to give and consider advice • Discussion about hypothetical situations • *Keep talking:* Interview about hypothetical situations • "Find someone who" activity about accomplishments
Interactions: Beginning instructions Continuing instructions Ending instructions	**Listening:** How things work Song dedications **Pronunciation:** Syllable stress	**Reading:** "Richie Starr" A fan site **Writing:** A music review	• Guessing game about music • *Keep talking:* Discussion about music • Information exchange with instructions • "Find someone who" activity about recent actions • *Keep talking:* "Find the differences" activity about two friends • Information exchange about songs and memories
Interactions: Asking about preferences Reminding someone of something	**Listening:** Hostel check-in A white-water rafting trip **Pronunciation:** Reduction of verbs	**Reading:** "A Taste of Cairo" A food blog **Writing:** A walking tour	• Interview about vacation activities • *Keep talking:* Comparison of travel preferences • Role play about checking into a hotel • Discussion about extreme sports • *Keep talking:* Plan for a backpacking trip • Information exchange about dream trips

Classroom language

A 🔊 Complete the conversations with the correct sentences. Then listen and check your answers.

What page are we on?	✓Excuse me. I'm very sorry I'm late.
Can you repeat that, please?	May I go to the restroom, please?
What's our homework?	Which role do you want to play?

A: *Excuse me. I'm very sorry I'm late.*

B: That's OK. Next time try to arrive on time.

A: _____

B: Thirteen. We're doing the Warm-up for Unit 2.

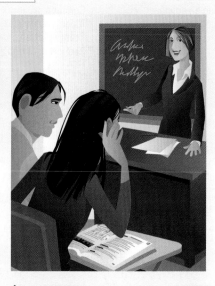

A: _____

B: Yes. I said, "Please work with a partner."

A: _____

B: I'll be Student A. You can be Student B.

A: _____

B: No problem. Please try to be quick.

A: _____

B: Please complete the activities for Unit 2 in your workbook.

B Pair work Practice the conversations.

2

Personalities

LESSON **A**	LESSON **B**	LESSON **C**	LESSON **D**
• Personality traits • Adverbs modifying adjectives and verbs	• Giving an opinion • Asking for agreement	• More personality traits • Present perfect with *for* and *since*	• Reading: "The Signs of the Zodiac" • Writing: My personality

Warm-up

A Describe the people in the picture. Where are they? What are they doing?

B What do you think each person is like? Why?

A You're extremely curious.

1 Vocabulary Personality traits

A 🔊 Match the adjectives and the sentences. Then listen and check your answers.

1. adventurous _____
2. ambitious _____
3. careful _____
4. curious _____
5. easygoing _____
6. optimistic _____
7. outgoing _____
8. stubborn _____

a. I'm interested in learning about people and things around me.
b. I'm friendly, and I like people.
c. I set high goals for myself.
d. I look on the bright side of things.
e. I do things slowly and with attention to detail.
f. I don't like to change my mind.
g. I am relaxed, and I don't worry about little things.
h. I love trying new, exciting activities.

B Pair work Describe people you know with each personality trait.
Tell your partner.

"My baby brother is very curious about the world. He wants to touch everything."

2 Language in context Are you a believer?

A 🔊 Read the personality descriptions. Underline the positive personality traits, and circle the negative ones.

Are you adventurous?

Answer ten questions in this quick personality test to find out just how adventurous you are!

Click here to begin.

Year of the Monkey
Born in years 1968, 1980, 1992, and 2004
You're extremely curious and outgoing. You solve problems well, but you can be stubborn about some things.

Personality Test Results
Your score: **13**
You're very adventurous, but you're not a very careful person. Try not to make decisions quickly. Take time to consider your options seriously.

Your Birth Order
As the first-born child in your family, you are a natural leader. You're pretty ambitious and like to work hard. However, you don't work well without direction.

B What about you? Do you believe the things in Part A can tell you about your personality? Why or why not?

3 Grammar 🔊 Adverbs modifying adjectives and verbs

Adverbs that modify adjectives come before the adjectives.	Adverbs that modify verbs go after the verb or the verb and its object.
You're **pretty** ambitious.	You don't work **well** without direction.
You're **extremely** curious and outgoing.	Try not to make decisions **quickly**.

Turn to page 152 for a list of adjective and adverb formations.

A Add the adverbs to the sentences. Then compare with a partner.

            slowly
1. I move ⌃ in the morning. (slowly)

2. I'm serious about my studies. (really)

3. I choose my words. (carefully)

4. I arrive at important meetings. (early)

5. My friends are important to me. (extremely)

6. I work in large groups. (well)

7. I'm optimistic about the future. (very)

8. It's easy for me to share my feelings. (fairly)

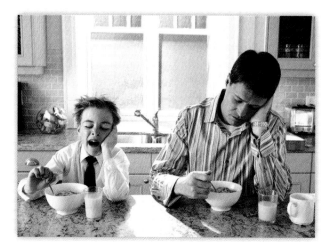

B Pair work Which sentences in Part A are true for you? Tell your partner.

4 Speaking My true self

A Pair work Interview your partner and ask questions for more information. Take notes.

	Name: _____	Yes	No	Extra information
1.	Are you very adventurous?	☐	☐	
2.	Do you make new friends easily?	☐	☐	
3.	Do you make decisions quickly?	☐	☐	
4.	Are you really stubborn about anything?	☐	☐	
5.	Do you work and study hard?	☐	☐	
6.	Do you get to class early?	☐	☐	
7.	Are you completely honest all the time?	☐	☐	

A: *Are you very adventurous?*
B: *Yes, I think so.*
A: *What's the most adventurous thing you've ever done?*

B Pair work Share the most interesting information with another partner.

5 Keep talking!

Go to page 137 for more practice.

I can talk about personality traits. ✓

B *In my opinion, . . .*

1 Interactions   Opinions

A Do you always tell people exactly what you think? Do you sometimes keep your opinions to yourself?

B 🔊 Listen to the conversation. Whose opinion do you agree with more? Then practice the conversation.

Fei: Have you seen Adam's new painting?

Ralph: Yes. I saw it last weekend.

Fei: It's not very good.

Ralph: No, it's not. He asked me what I thought of it. I said I didn't think it was his best painting.

Fei: You're kidding! How did he react?

Ralph: He didn't seem very happy to hear that. But he did ask.

Fei: In my opinion, it's better to say something positive, even if you don't really mean it. Don't you agree?

Ralph: I don't know. Why do you say that?

Fei: Well, it's not always easy to hear the truth.

Ralph: I'm not so sure. I find that honesty is always the best policy.

C 🔊 Read the expressions below. Complete each box with a similar expression from the conversation. Then listen and check your answers.

Giving an opinion	*Asking for agreement*
_____	_____
If you ask me, . . .	Don't you think so?
Maybe it's just me, but I think . . .	Don't you think that's true?

D Pair work Check (✓) the opinions you agree with. Then ask your partner for agreement.

1. ☐ Women are more stubborn than men.
   ☐ Men are more stubborn than women.

2. ☐ It's never OK to lie.
   ☐ It's sometimes OK to lie.

3. ☐ A small group of friends is better than a large group of friends.
   ☐ A large group of friends is better than a small group of friends.

2 **Pronunciation** Reduction of *don't you*

A 🔊 Listen and repeat. Notice how *don't you* is pronounced /dountʃə/.

Don't you agree?   Don't you think so?   Don't you think that's true?

B **Pair work** Say the opinions in Exercise 1D again. Ask your partner for agreement. Reduce *don't you* to /dountʃə/.

3 **Listening** A book of proverbs

A 🔊 Listen to Tina and Cal talk about proverbs. Number the proverbs from 1 to 4 in the order you hear them.

Proverbs	Does Tina agree?	Does Cal agree?
☐ Practice makes perfect.	yes / no	yes / no
☐ Better late than never.	yes / no	yes / no
☐ Beauty is only skin deep.	yes / no	yes / no
☐ Two heads are better than one.	yes / no	yes / no

B 🔊 Listen again. Do Tina and Cal agree with the proverbs in Part A? Circle *yes* or *no*.

C **Pair work** Do you agree with each proverb? Why or why not? Do you know any similar proverbs in your own language? Tell your partner.

4 **Speaking** Don't you think so?

A What's your opinion? Circle the words.

1. People are **more** / **less** ambitious these days.
2. Young people are **more** / **less** optimistic than older people.
3. **First-born** / **Last-born** children are usually very easygoing.
4. It's **possible** / **impossible** to change your personality.

B **Group work** Discuss your opinions from Part A.

> A: *If you ask me, people are less ambitious these days. Don't you think so?*
> B: *I'm not so sure. Why do you say that?*
> C: *Well, maybe it's just me, but I feel no one wants to work hard these days.*
> D: *I'm not sure I really agree. In my opinion, . . .*

C **Group work** Think of three other topics. Share your opinions about them. Does anyone agree with you?

"In my opinion, people worry about their appearance too much. Don't you agree?"

I can *give an opinion.* ☑
I can *ask for agreement.* ☑

C *We've been friends for six years.*

1 Vocabulary More personality traits

A 🔊 Match the adjectives and the definitions. Then listen and check your answers.

1. agreeable _____	a. thinking of the needs of others
2. considerate _____	b. treating people equally or right
3. decisive _____	c. friendly and pleasing
4. fair _____	d. making decisions quickly

5. honest _____	e. waiting without getting annoyed
6. mature _____	f. doing what is expected or promised
7. patient _____	g. truthful
8. reliable _____	h. behaving in a responsible way

B 🔊 Complete the chart with the opposites of the words in Part A. Then listen and check your answers.

dis-	im-	in-	un-
disagreeable			

C Pair work What are the three best personality traits to have in a friend? What are the three worst? Discuss your ideas.

2 Conversation Time to say you're sorry

A 🔊 Listen to the conversation. How does Lance describe Jill's reaction?

Lance: I don't know what to do about my friend Jill. I haven't spoken to her since last weekend, and she won't answer my text messages.

Emily: Did something happen?

Lance: Yeah. I said something about her to another friend. She found out, and now I feel terrible. To be honest, it wasn't anything serious, though. I think she's being unfair and a little immature.

Emily: Well, put yourself in her shoes. Imagine a friend saying something about you behind your back.

Lance: You're probably right.

Emily: Have you been friends for a long time?

Lance: Yes. We've been friends for six years, and we used to talk all the time.

Emily: Then I think you should do the considerate thing and call to say you're sorry.

B 🔊 Listen to Lance and Jill's phone conversation. What word does Lance use to describe himself?

3 Grammar 🔊 | Present perfect with *for* and *since*

Use the present perfect to describe an action that began in the past and continues to now. Use for *to specify the amount of time. Use* since *to specify the starting point.*

How long have you been friends?
  We've been friends **for six years**.
  We've been friends **since middle school**.
She's been upset **for several days**.
I haven't spoken to her **since last weekend**.

for	*since*
ten minutes	3:00
two hours	last night
several days	Monday
a month	October
six years	2009
a long time	high school
quite a while	I was a kid

A Complete the sentences with *for* or *since*. Then compare with a partner.

1. Rod has become more considerate _____ he got married.
2. Mr. and Mrs. Kim haven't had an argument _____ 1981.
3. Pete and Lisa have been on the phone _____ six hours.
4. Tim hasn't spoken with his brother _____ a long time.
5. Jay's been totally unreliable _____ he started his new job.
6. Inez has been in her new job _____ three months.
7. Annie has become less immature _____ high school.
8. Jessica and Hector have been married _____ 25 years.

B Pair work Ask and answer the questions.

1. How long have you been in this class?
2. What haven't you done since you were a kid?
3. What have you wanted to do for a long time?

4 Speaking Three friends

A Think of three friends. Complete the chart.

	Names	How long we've been friends	Their personality traits
1.			
2.			
3.			

B Group work Tell your group about your friends. Use your information from Part A. Ask and answer questions for more information.

  A: *I've known my friend Jesse since middle school.*
  B: *What's he like?*
  A: *He's very honest and reliable.*

5 Keep talking!

Go to page 138 for more practice.

I can describe people's personalities. ☑

D What is your personality?

1 Reading 🔊

A When were you born? Read the description of your zodiac sign.
Does it describe you well?

cambridge.org/thesignsofthezodiac

THE SIGNS OF THE ZODIAC

 CAPRICORN Dec. 22 – Jan. 20
You're ambitious and good at business, but you sometimes worry about things too much.

 CANCER June 22 – July 22
You're very patient and want everyone to get along, but you can have difficulty showing your feelings.

 AQUARIUS Jan. 21 – Feb. 19
You're creative and care about other people's feelings, but you can sometimes be difficult to work with.

 LEO July 23 – Aug. 23
You're a leader. You like to give, but you don't like to ask for things. You're not very patient.

 PISCES Feb. 20 – March 20
You're considerate, but sometimes you don't help yourself enough. You decide things quickly and rarely change your mind.

 VIRGO Aug. 24 – Sept. 22
You're ambitious and want things done with no mistakes. You are not always open to new ideas.

 ARIES March 21 – April 20
You're optimistic and creative. You know what you want, but you sometimes have difficulty sharing your feelings.

 LIBRA Sept. 23 – Oct. 22
You get along with everyone and are curious about many things. You're always looking for something better.

 TAURUS April 21 – May 21
You're talkative and always say exactly what you think. You work hard, but you can get angry quickly.

 SCORPIO Oct. 23 – Nov. 21
You're a reliable friend, but you can have difficulty sharing your feelings. You know exactly what you want.

 GEMINI May 22 – June 21
You like adventure. You love to try new things and can be very creative. You can sometimes be unreliable.

 SAGITTARIUS Nov. 22 – Dec. 21
You're honest – sometimes *too* honest. You don't always learn from your mistakes.

B Read the chart. Complete the sentences with the correct zodiac signs.

1. A _____ hates asking for things.
2. A _____ talks a lot.
3. A _____ is good at business.
4. A _____ wants everything perfect.
5. A _____ is adventurous.
6. A _____ is decisive.
7. A _____ always tells the truth.
8. A _____ is difficult to work with.

C **Group work** Think of three people you know. What is each person's zodiac sign? Does it describe their personalities well? Tell your group.

2 **Listening** Imagine you're in a forest . . .

A 🔊 Listen to the personality test. Number the questions from 1 to 7 in the order you hear them.

☐ What's it made of? _____

☐ Who are you with? _____

☐ What do you do with it? _____

☐ How big is it? _____

☐ What kind do you see? _____

☐ What's on the table? _____

☐ Is it open or closed? _____

B 🔊 Listen again. Now take the personality test. Answer the questions with your own ideas.

C Pair work Compare your answers. Then turn to page 153 to see what your answers mean.

3 **Writing and speaking** My personality

A Think about your personality. Answer the questions.

- What are your positive personality traits? _____
- Are there any traits you'd like to change? _____
- Has your personality changed through the years? If so, how? _____

_____

B Write a paragraph about your personality, but do not write your name! Use the model and your answers in Part A to help you.

What Am I Like?
I'm a pretty easygoing and outgoing
person. I'm also very optimistic about
the future. I think people like to be
around me. However, I can be stubborn
sometimes. . . .

C Group work Put your papers facedown on the table. Take one paper and read the description. Your group guesses who it is and agrees or disagrees with the description. Take turns.

A: *I think that paragraph describes Dana.*
B: *Yes, that's right. I wrote that one.*
C: *I agree you're easygoing, Dana, but I don't really think you're stubborn.*
B: *Yes, I am!*

I can talk about my personality. ☑

Wrap-up

1 Quick pair review

Lesson A Test your partner! Say an adjective. Can your partner write the adverb form correctly? Take turns. You have two minutes.

"Careful."

1. *carefully*   3. _____   5. _____
2. _____   4. _____   6. _____

Lesson B Give your opinion! Look at the two pieces of art. What do you think of them? Give two opinions about each one. You have two minutes.

A: *If you ask me, I think the sculpture is weird. Don't you think so?*
B: *In my opinion, it's very interesting.*

Lesson C Brainstorm! Make a list of positive and negative personality traits. How many do you know? You have two minutes.

Lesson D Find out! Who are two people that you and your partner know with the same personality traits? You have two minutes.

A: *My friend John is really stubborn. Do you know a stubborn person?*
B: *Yes. My little sister!*

2 In the real world

What's your zodiac sign? Find your horoscope from yesterday or last week in an English-language newspaper, magazine, or website. Was it true? Write about it.

> *My Horoscope*
> *I'm a Pisces. My horoscope last week said,*
> *"You are going to have a difficult day at*
> *work." It was true. I was very busy and*
> *nervous because I had to give a presentation.*
> *Luckily, it went very well!*

The environment

LESSON A
- Environmental impacts
- Quantifiers

LESSON B
- Giving an approximate answer
- Avoiding answering

LESSON C
- Tips to help the environment
- First conditional

LESSON D
- Reading: "One-of-a-Kind Homes"
- Writing: Local concerns

Warm-up

A Look at the "before" and "after" pictures. What do you see? What has changed?

B Which was the biggest improvement? Which was the easiest to do? Which was the most difficult?

A Going green

1 Vocabulary Environmental impacts

A 🔊 Label the pictures with the correct words. Then listen and check your answers.

| e-waste | hybrid car | organic food | pollution | solar energy |
| global warming | nuclear energy | plastic bags | recycling bin | wind farm |

1. _____ 2. _____ 3. _____ 4. _____ 5. _____

6. _____ 7. _____ 8. _____ 9. _____ 10. _____

B Pair work How do the things in Part A impact the environment?

2 Language in context Green products

A 🔊 Read the ads. What makes each product "green"?

GET GREEN GOODS! HOME **PRODUCTS** SERVICES CONTACT

Compact fluorescent lightbulbs
Regular bulbs waste too much energy, so why not use compact fluorescent lightbulbs (CFLs)? They use less energy, and you save more money in the long term.
$20 for a pack of 3

Cloth shopping bag
Who needs paper or plastic? Bring your own cloth bag to the grocery store or mall. This bag makes an important statement and is made of 100% organic cotton.
$5

Recycled toothbrush
Made from 100% recyclable plastic, each toothbrush comes with a reusable travel case. Junior toothbrushes feature endangered animals.
$20 for a pack of 6, or $18 for a pack of 6 Junior toothbrushes

Steel water bottle
Why should we use fewer plastic water bottles? Because too many of them end up in landfills and cause pollution. It's cool to carry your own reusable bottle.
$15

B What about you? Do you own any green products? Would you buy these?

3 Grammar ◄)) Quantifiers

Quantifiers with count nouns
We need **more** wind farms.
There are**n't enough** recycling bins.
There are **too many** bottles in landfills.
People should buy **fewer** plastic bottles.

Quantifiers with noncount nouns
You save **more** money with CFLs.
People do**n't** buy **enough** organic food.
Regular lightbulbs use **too much** energy.
People should try to use **less** plastic.

A Complete the opinions with quantifiers. Then compare with a partner.

1. "I think it's good that _____ people are buying hybrid cars. They help reduce global warming."
2. "In my opinion, there's _____ e-waste in our landfills. We need better and safer ways to recycle electronics."
3. "Farmers should grow _____ organic food. I prefer food without chemicals."
4. "Unfortunately, not _____ people use solar power. Is it because it's expensive?"
5. "I feel people should use _____ nuclear energy. Isn't it dangerous?"
6. "Some people say they don't have _____ time to recycle. That's crazy!"
7. "Maybe it's just me, but I think shoppers should take _____ plastic and paper bags from the supermarket. I always bring my own bags."
8. "_____ people throw plastic bottles in garbage cans. They should use recycling bins."

B Pair work Do you agree with the opinions in Part A? Why or why not? Tell your partner.

4 Pronunciation Stress in compound nouns

A ◄)) Listen and repeat. Notice how the first noun in compound nouns often receives stronger stress.

landfill   **light**bulb   **travel** case   **water** bottle

B Pair work Practice the compound nouns. Stress the first noun.

toothbrush   garbage can   recycling bin   wind farm

5 Speaking Our community

A Pair work What environmental problems does your community have? Complete the sentences.

1. There's too much _____ .
2. There isn't enough _____ .
3. We should have fewer _____ .
4. There are too many _____ .
5. There aren't enough _____ .
6. We should use less _____ .

B Group work Share your ideas with another pair. Did you identify the same problems? Which are the most important?

6 Keep talking!

Go to page 139 for more practice.

I can discuss environmental problems. ☑

B I'd rather not say.

1 Interactions · Answering and avoiding answering

A Imagine these people are asking you questions. Are there any questions they might ask you that you think are too personal and that you would not answer?

| a doctor | a friend | a neighbor | a parent | a stranger | a teacher |

B 🔊 Listen to the conversation. What question doesn't Jim answer? Then practice the conversation.

Carl: So, Jim, how's the new car?

Jim: Hey, Carl. It's great. I'm really happy with it.

Carl: It's a hybrid, isn't it?

Jim: Yeah. It causes less pollution. I'm trying to do my part to help the environment, you know?

Carl: That's great. How long have you had it?

Jim: I've only had it for a week.

Carl: Really? How many kilometers have you driven?

Jim: I'd say about 150.

Carl: So, how does it run?

Jim: Oh, it runs very well. I'll give you a ride later if you want.

Carl: OK, thanks. How much did it cost, exactly?

Jim: Actually, I'd rather not say. But I know I made a good purchase.

C 🔊 Read the expressions below. Complete each box with a similar expression from the conversation. Then listen and check your answers.

Giving an approximate answer

_____
I'd say maybe . . .
Probably . . .

Avoiding answering

_____
I'd prefer not to say.
I'd rather not answer that.

D Match the questions and the responses. Then practice with a partner.

1. How often do you drive? _____
2. How much do you drive every day? _____
3. How many people have you given rides to? _____
4. How much did you sell your old car for? _____

a. I'd say about ten.
b. Probably five or six times a week.
c. I'd rather not answer that.
d. I'd say about 30 minutes.

2 Listening Consumer research

A 🔊 Listen to a man answer survey questions in a grocery store. Number the questions from 1 to 9 in the order you hear them.

☐ Have your buying habits changed in the last year? _____

1️⃣ How often do you walk to the grocery store? *All the time.* _____

☐ Do you usually ask for paper or plastic bags? _____

☐ How much do you spend on groceries every month? _____

☐ How many people are there in your household? _____

☐ What is the highest level of education you've completed? _____

☐ What do you do for a living? _____

☐ Do you ever shop for groceries online? _____

☐ How often do you buy environmentally friendly products? _____

B 🔊 Listen again. Write the man's answers.

C Pair work Ask and answer the questions in Part A. Answer with your own information, or avoid answering.

3 Speaking Do you waste water?

A Read the survey. Are there any questions you would avoid answering, or is there any information you wouldn't share?

WATER USE SURVEY

Name: _____   Phone number: _____

Address: _____   Email: _____

Age: _____   Education: _____

How many showers do you take in a week? _____

How long do you spend in the shower? _____

Do you ever leave the water running when you brush your teeth? _____

Do you wash dishes by hand or use a dishwasher? _____

When you wash dishes, do you leave the water running? _____

When you wash clothes, is the washing machine always completely full? _____

Do you flush the toilet after every use? _____

B Pair work Interview your partner. Complete the survey with his or her answers. Mark an ✗ if he or she avoids answering.

C Pair work Compare your answers. Who uses more water? How could you use less water?

I *can* give an approximate answer. ☑

I *can* avoid answering. ☑

C What will happen?

1 Vocabulary Tips to help the environment

A 🔊 Match the tips and the pictures. Then listen and check your answers.

a. Buy local food.	d. Pay bills online.	g. Use cloth shopping bags.
b. Fix leaky faucets.	e. Take public transportation.	h. Use rechargeable batteries.
c. Grow your own food.	f. Use a clothesline.	

 1. ☐
 2. ☐
 3. ☐
 4. ☐

 5. ☐
 6. ☐
 7. ☐
 8. ☐

B Pair work Which things in Part A do you do now? Which don't you do? Tell your partner.

2 Conversation This is awful!

A 🔊 Listen to the conversation. When does Kendra want to start taking public transportation?

Ina: This is awful! It's taking forever to get to work.

Kendra: I know. There are just too many cars these days! The traffic seems to get worse and worse.

Ina: Maybe we should start taking public transportation. If we take the subway, we won't have to sit in traffic.

Kendra: And we might save money if we take the subway.

Ina: I think you're right. Also, if we take public transportation, we won't get stressed out before work. So, when do we start?

Kendra: How about tomorrow?

B 🔊 Listen to their conversation the next day. What are they unhappy about?

3 Grammar 🔊 **First conditional**

First conditional sentences describe real possibilities. Use the present tense in the if *clause (the condition). Use* will *in the main clause.*

If we **take** public transportation, we**'ll save** money.

If we **take** public transportation, we **won't get** stressed out.

Air pollution **will get** worse if we **don't reduce** the number of cars.

Use modals such as may, might, *or* could *in the main clause when you're less certain about the results.*

If air pollution **gets** worse, more people **may get** sick.

If you **don't fix** your leaky faucet, you **might get** a high water bill.

You **could spend** money on other things if you **grow** your own food.

A Write first conditional sentences with the two clauses. Then compare with a partner.

1. you'll use 60 percent less energy / you replace your regular lightbulbs with CFLs

   You'll use 60 percent less energy if you replace your regular lightbulbs with CFLs.

2. you pay your bills online / you'll use less paper

   _____

3. we fix our leaky faucets / we'll save water

   _____

4. there won't be much air pollution / everyone uses hybrid cars

   _____

5. you use a clothesline / other people may start to do the same

   _____

6. we use rechargeable batteries / we could save a lot of money

   _____

B Pair work What else will or may happen for each condition in Part A? Discuss your ideas.

> A: *What else will happen if you replace your regular lightbulbs with CFLs?*
> B: *If I replace my regular lightbulbs with CFLs, I'll have cheaper electric bills.*

4 Speaking Around the circle

A Write a sentence about what will happen if you change a habit to become greener.

If I grow my own food, I will eat better.

B Group work Sit in a circle. Go around the circle and share your ideas. Repeat your classmates' main clauses as conditions, and add new ideas.

> A: *If I grow my own food, I will eat better.*
> B: *If you eat better, you will feel healthier.*
> C: *If you feel healthier, you won't need to go to the doctor very often.*

5 Keep talking!

Go to page 140 for more practice.

Go to page 140 for more practice.

I can talk about future possibilities. ☑

D *Finding solutions*

1 Reading

A Look at the pictures. Which home would you prefer to live in? Why?

B Read the article. Write the captions under the correct pictures.

| The Recycled-Tire House | The Found-Object House | The Greenhouse |

One-of-a-Kind HOMES

Shoichi wanted to live in an environmentally friendly home, and he always liked the greenhouses in his neighborhood in Tokyo, Japan. So he decided to create his own greenhouse-style home. Sunlight warms his new home, and a plastic cover around the house helps to keep the heat inside. There aren't any walls or rooms. The "rooms" are actually large boxes on wheels. He can move them anywhere he likes, even outside. He loves his home, but sometimes he would like to be able to move the whole house.

Ruth is an artist who lives in the Rocky Mountains in the U.S. state of Colorado. Over the years, she found and collected a lot of old objects for her art. When she decided she wanted to live in a more unusual home, she had a creative idea. She would use many of the old materials that she collected in the home's design. For example, she used old car parts in the front door and tire rubber as the roof. She also used the door of an old car as part of a wall, so she can still lower the window!

Wayne and Cate are a couple from the U.S. state of Montana. They wanted a new home that wasn't too expensive. Their solution was simple – they built their own home. They recycled and used 250 old tires as the base of the house and old glass for the windows. They even used 13,000 empty soda cans in the house. Their home also has large windows and lots of plants and flowers. Solar energy keeps the house warm, even on cold days.

C Read the article again. Answer the questions.

1. What warms the inside of Shoichi's home? _____
2. What would Shoichi like to be able to do? _____
3. What creative idea did Ruth have? _____
4. Where are there car parts in Ruth's home? _____
5. Why did Wayne and Cate build their own home? _____
6. What did Wayne and Cate use to build their home? _____

D Pair work Have you heard of or seen any unique homes or buildings? Were they environmentally friendly? Tell your partner.

2 **Listening** Award winners

A 🔊 Listen to the conversations about two award winners, Gabriela McCall and Tayler McGillis. Who do the phrases below describe? Write T (Tayler) or G (Gabriela).

1. _T_ raised money for local charities.
2. ____ is a student in Puerto Rico.
3. ____ won an award at age 12.
4. ____ collects and recycles cans.
5. ____ helps birds.
6. ____ teaches children.
7. ____ speaks at schools about recycling.
8. ____ took photos to start a project.

Tayler McGillis   Gabriela McCall

B 🔊 Listen again. Correct the false sentences.

1. Tayler raised more than ~~$900~~ for local charities. _$9,000_

2. Tayler's new goal is to collect 175,000 bottles every year. _____

3. Gabriela's project helps protect the ocean for birds in Puerto Rico. _____

4. Gabriela teaches children about recycling so that they respect the environment. _____

3 **Writing and speaking** Local concerns

A Write a letter to a local official about an environmental problem in your community. Use the questions and the model to help you.

- What is the problem?
- Who or what does the problem affect?
- Who or what is causing it?
- What's a solution to the problem?

Dear City Councilman,

I am a student. I am writing to tell you about the amount of noise near our school. There is a lot of construction work and traffic near our school. It is very difficult for us to study and learn during the day.

I have an idea for a possible solution to this problem. If . . .

B Group work Share your letters. Do you think the solutions will solve the problems? Can you offer other solutions?

C Class activity What are the most important concerns in your community? Who else can you write to or talk to about your concerns?

> *I can discuss solutions to problems.* ✓

Wrap-up

1 Quick pair review

Lesson A Brainstorm! Make a list of environmentally friendly products.
How many do you know? You have two minutes.

Lesson B Do you remember? Is the sentence giving an approximate
answer, or is it avoiding answering? Write AP (approximate answer) or
AV (avoiding answering). You have one minute.

How much did your car cost?		How much trash do you throw away a week?	
I'd say about $3,000.	_____	I'd rather not answer that.	_____
I'd prefer not to say.	_____	I'd rather not say.	_____
I'd say maybe $6,000.	_____	Probably about five bags.	_____

Lesson C Give your opinion! What do you think? Complete the
sentences together. You have three minutes.

1. Our city will get cleaner if _____ .
2. If our school uses solar energy, _____ .
3. If we eat organic food, _____ .
4. We could recycle more if _____ .

Lesson D Find out! Who is one person you know who does each thing?
You have two minutes.

- Who uses environmentally friendly products at home?
- Who takes public transportation to work?
- Who has taught you about an environmental issue?

A: *My aunt has solar panels on the roof of her house.*
B: *My father uses compact fluorescent lightbulbs.*

2 In the real world

How can we solve this? Go online and find information in English that gives
solutions to one of these problems. Then write about them.

pollution from cars	pollution from factories
global warming	too much garbage

> *Our Pollution Problem*
> If more people have hybrid cars, there will be
> less pollution. People can also carpool. If we
> share rides, there will be fewer cars on the road.
> Also, if we . . .

Relationships

LESSON **A**	LESSON **B**	LESSON **C**	LESSON **D**
• Relationship behaviors • Expressions with infinitives	• Apologizing • Accepting an apology	• Inseparable phrasal verbs • Modals for speculating	• Reading: "Addy's Advice" • Writing: A piece of advice

Warm-up

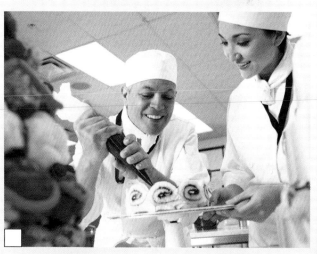

A What is the relationship between the people? Number the pictures.

1. brother and sister   2. neighbors   3. co-workers   4. friends

B What do you think is happening in each picture? Do they all have good relationships?

A Healthy relationships

1 Vocabulary Relationship behaviors

A 🔊 Match the words and the sentences. Then listen and check your answers.

1. apologize _____	a. No! I'm not listening to you.
2. argue _____	b. I think we really need to talk about it.
3. communicate _____	c. I'm really sorry. I didn't mean to hurt your feelings.

4. compromise _____	d. I know you're sorry. It's OK.
5. criticize _____	e. Why don't I wash the dishes and you do the laundry?
6. forgive _____	f. You're being unfair. It's your turn to take out the garbage.

7. gossip _____	g. I told her I liked her new dress, but I didn't.
8. judge _____	h. Others may disagree, but I think what you said was awful.
9. lie _____	i. Did you hear about Wendy? You'll never guess what I heard.

B Pair work Which actions from Part A should people do to have healthy relationships? Which shouldn't they do? Discuss your ideas.

2 Language in context Relationship tips

A 🔊 Read the relationship tips. Why is it a bad idea to criticize someone in front of others?

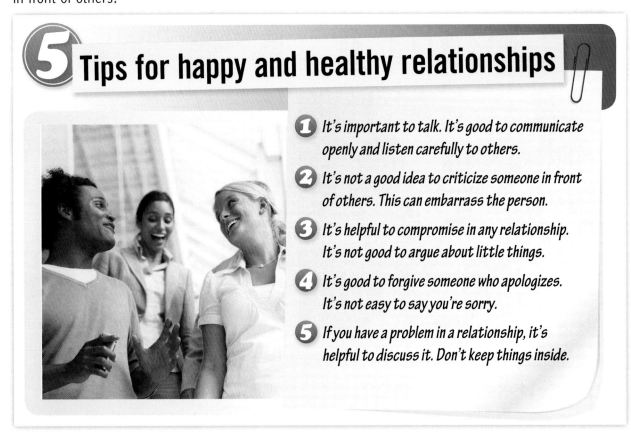

5 Tips for happy and healthy relationships

1 It's important to talk. It's good to communicate openly and listen carefully to others.

2 It's not a good idea to criticize someone in front of others. This can embarrass the person.

3 It's helpful to compromise in any relationship. It's not good to argue about little things.

4 It's good to forgive someone who apologizes. It's not easy to say you're sorry.

5 If you have a problem in a relationship, it's helpful to discuss it. Don't keep things inside.

B What about you? Do you agree with all the tips? Why or why not?

3 Grammar 🔊 Expressions with infinitives

Use infinitives after It's + *an adjective.*

It's good **to forgive** someone.   It's not good **to argue**.

It's important **to talk**.   It's never helpful **to judge** someone.

You can also use infinitives after It's + *a noun phrase.*

It's a good idea **to accept** an apology.   It's not a good idea **to criticize** someone.

A Circle the infinitives for the best relationship advice. Then compare with a partner.

1. It's important **to lie** / **to communicate** in a relationship.
2. It's helpful **to share** / **to forget** your feelings when you have a problem.
3. It's nice **to gossip** / **to think** about other people before making decisions.
4. It's a good idea **to judge** / **to meet** new people.
5. It's useful **to discuss** / **to accept** problems.
6. It's not a good idea **to argue** / **to compromise** with your friends a lot.

B Pair work Complete the sentences with your own ideas. Use *It's* expressions. Then discuss them.

1. _____ to be a reliable friend.
2. _____ to be honest with your parents.
3. _____ to apologize to someone but not really mean it.
4. _____ to say something if a friend is gossiping about you.

4 Pronunciation Sentence stress

A 🔊 Listen and repeat. Notice the stress on the important words in the sentences.

It's **important** to **talk**.   It's **not good** to **argue** about **little things**.

B 🔊 Listen to the sentences. Underline the stressed words.

It's helpful to compromise.   It's not easy to say you're sorry.

5 Speaking Good advice?

A Pair work Choose a relationship from the list below. Then make a list of the five most important tips to make the relationship happy and healthy. Discuss your ideas.

best friends	co-workers
a brother and sister	a married couple
a child and parent	a teacher and student

B Group work Share your tips with another pair. What's the best piece of advice you heard?

6 Keep talking!

Go to page 141 for more practice.

I can discuss what's important in relationships.

B *I'm really sorry.*

1 Interactions   Apologizing

A Is it difficult for you to say you're sorry? Can you remember the last thing you apologized for?

B 🔊 Listen to the conversation. What excuse does Susan give Gina? Then practice the conversation.

> **Gina:** Hello?
> **Susan:** Gina?
> **Gina:** Yeah.
> **Susan:** Hi. It's Susan.
> **Gina:** Hi, Susan.
> **Susan:** Listen, I know I missed your party last night. I'm sorry.
> **Gina:** Oh, that's OK. Is everything OK?
> **Susan:** Yeah, but you'll never believe what happened. It's kind of embarrassing. I mixed up the date.
> **Gina:** What do you mean?
> **Susan:** I thought the party was on the 31st, not the 30th.
> **Gina:** Oh, I see.
> **Susan:** So, how was the party?
> **Gina:** It was great. But we missed you!

C 🔊 Read the expressions below. Complete each box with a similar expression from the conversation. Then listen and check your answers.

Apologizing

_____
I'm really sorry.
My apologies.

Accepting an apology

_____
Don't worry about it.
There's no need to apologize.

D Number the sentences from 1 to 7. Then practice with a partner.

_____ **A:** I'm really sorry I didn't meet you at the café yesterday.

_____ **A:** Hi. It's Greg.

_____ **A:** Well, the repairs will be very expensive.

_____ **A:** My car broke down, and I forgot my phone.

_____ **B:** Is your car OK?

_____ **B:** Don't worry about it.

_____ **B:** Oh. Hi, Greg.

2 Listening What happened?

A 🔊 Listen to four people apologize over the phone. What happened? Where did they *not* go? Number the pictures from 1 to 4.

B 🔊 Listen again. Complete the excuses with the correct information.

1. I was at the _____ and completely forgot the _____ .
2. I washed my _____ last night, and the _____ was in my pocket.
3. I was out of _____ . My grandmother was in the _____ .
4. I'm in a _____ at work. I can't _____ right now.

C Pair work Are all the excuses good ones? Would you accept each person's apology? Discuss your ideas.

3 Speaking Explain yourself!

A Read the situations. Write an excuse for each one. Be creative!

Situations	Excuses
You are 30 minutes late for your own wedding.	
You missed your dentist appointment.	
You didn't bring your résumé to a job interview.	
You forgot to pick up your friend.	
You didn't do your English homework.	
You broke your classmate's cell phone.	

B Pair work Role-play the situations. Then change roles.

Student A: Apologize to Student B for each situation in Part A. Then make an excuse.

Student B: Ask Student A to explain each situation. Then accept the apology.

I can apologize and give excuses. ✓
I can accept an apology. ✓

C That can't be the problem.

1 Vocabulary Inseparable phrasal verbs

A 🔊 Match the sentences. Then listen and check your answers.

1. It's awful when people **break up**. _____	a. They should call before they visit.
2. I need friends that I can **count on**. _____	b. It's always better to stay together.
3. It's not nice when friends just **drop by**. _____	c. My best friends are all reliable.

4. My family and I **get along** well. _____	d. They can be so immature.
5. My friends and I love to **get together**. _____	e. We meet every Saturday.
6. Most teenagers need to **grow up**. _____	f. We hardly ever argue.

7. People used to **pick on** me in class. _____	g. I sometimes see them at the coffee shop.
8. I love to **run into** old friends. _____	h. I'm just like her.
9. I **take after** my mother. _____	i. They were mean to me.

B Pair work Which sentences do you agree with or are true for you?
Tell your partner.

> **A:** *I agree that it's awful when people break up, but I disagree that it's always better to stay together.*
> **B:** *I agree with you. Some people shouldn't stay together when they argue a lot.*

2 Conversation He must be really busy.

A 🔊 Listen to the conversation. What is Evan probably doing right now?

Ryan: My friend Evan never seems to have time for me these days. I just can't count on him anymore.

Katie: Well, he started a new job, right? He must be really busy.

Ryan: Yeah, I'm sure he is. But he used to drop by or call me all the time.

Katie: He might be feeling stressed out from the job. Or he could be upset with you about something.

Ryan: No, that can't be the problem. I haven't done anything wrong. I think I'd better call him.

Katie: Yeah, I think you should.

Ryan: OK. . . . Well, there's no answer.

Katie: He must still be sleeping. It's only 6:30!

B 🔊 Listen to Ryan call Evan later in the day. What was the real problem with Evan?

3 Grammar 🔊 Modals for speculating

Speculating with more certainty

He **must be** really busy. He started a new job.

He **must not leave** his house very often. He always seems to be busy.

He **can't be** upset with me. I haven't done anything to him.

Speculating with less certainty

He **could be** upset about something. Maybe you did something to him.

He **may not like** his new job. I haven't heard how he likes it.

He **might be feeling** stressed out. His new job may be a lot of work.

A Circle the correct words. Then compare with a partner.

1. I don't know his weekend plans. He **must / could** drop by on Saturday.
2. She didn't say much on the phone to him. They **must not / might** be getting along.
3. They **must / may not** come to the party. They're going out to dinner that night.
4. She **can't / could** take after her father. She's really tall, but he's pretty short.
5. You're coughing and sneezing so much. You **must / must not** be getting sick.
6. They **can't / might** be tired. Maybe they stayed up late to study for the test.

B Read the situations. Complete the sentences with your own ideas. Then compare with a partner.

1. Pamela and Miguel don't get along anymore. She doesn't want to talk about it.
   Pamela must _____ .
2. Jeff just ran into his college friend Mary. He hasn't seen her for 20 years.
   Jeff could _____ .
3. Luis and Teresa arranged to get together at a restaurant, but she never came.
   Teresa may not _____ .
4. Brian dropped by and asked to copy your homework. You're not going to give it to him. Brian might _____ .

4 Speaking Look around!

A Pair work Look around the classroom. Speculate about your classmates.

A: *I think Tom must be playing tennis later. He has his tennis racket with him today.*
B: *And Carmen might be happy about something. She's smiling a lot.*

B Class activity Were your speculations correct? Ask your classmates.

A: *Tom, I see you have your tennis racket. Are you playing tennis later?*
B: *Actually, no. I played before class.*

5 Keep talking!

Go to pages 142–143 for more practice.

I can speculate about people. ☑

D Getting advice

1 Reading ◄))

A Do you ever listen to talk shows on the radio or watch them on TV? What kind of problems do they usually discuss? Do people give good advice on the shows?

B Read the first few sentences of each email sent to the radio show *Addy's Advice*. Who does each person have a problem with?

○ ○ ○

ADDY'S ADVICE

1. I have a big problem. It's my best friend. She doesn't really have any time for me these days. I call her, and she can't talk. I text her, and she doesn't answer right away. I think it's because of her cat, Peaches. She got this little cat for her 30th birthday, and now she takes it everywhere. She even dresses it in little sweaters and hats. I don't know what to do. Is it possible to be jealous of a cat? – **T. J.**

2. There's this new person at work. She works next to me and we get along, but she's always asking me to do things for her. For example, she asks me to get her coffee when I get some for myself. Or she drops by and asks me to copy things for her when she's "busy." She's not my boss! Should I just refuse to do things for her? I want to be nice, but I have to do my own work. Can you help me, please? – **Marcy**

3. My little brother is driving me crazy. I'm 15, and he's 10. He has his own friends, but he won't leave me and my friends alone. They come over a lot to study or just watch TV. He bothers me and sometimes tells my friends things that are personal about me. Maybe he just wants attention, but it's very annoying. He should just grow up! Anyway, I told my mom and dad, but they say I need to solve the problem. – **Kathy**

4. I'm a neat person, and I used to live alone. I got a roommate a few months ago to help with the rent. The problem is, my roommate is not like me at all. He never does any chores around the house. He just sits around playing video games and watching TV. The apartment is always a mess, and I'm the one who has to clean it up. I can't count on him for anything. Should I just clean the apartment myself? This is a big problem for me. – **Daniel**

C Read the emails again. Who is each question about? Check (✓) the correct answers.

Who . . . ?	T. J.	Marcy	Kathy	Daniel
lives with a messy person				
is a teenager				
is jealous of an animal				
is doing someone else's work				
lived alone last year				
mentions parents in the letter				

D Pair work Have you ever had similar problems? What did you do about them? Tell your partner.

2 **Listening** On the air

A 🔊 Listen to the radio show *Addy's Advice*. What advice does Addy give to each person from Exercise 1? Check (✓) the correct answers.

1. ☐ Show interest in the cat.
   ☐ Get a cat of your own.
2. ☐ Write your co-worker a note.
   ☐ Ask your co-worker to do things.
3. ☐ Go to someone else's house.
   ☐ Remind your parents of the situation.
4. ☐ Throw the roommate out.
   ☐ Communicate.

B 🔊 Listen again. Which statements does Addy probably agree or disagree with? Write A (agree) or D (disagree).

1. People never lose interest in things over time. _____

2. Most people have problems with co-workers at some time. _____

3. Parents don't always need to solve their children's problems. _____

4. Look for a new roommate if you have a problem. _____

3 **Writing** A piece of advice

A Choose an email from Exercise 1. Think of three pieces of advice.

B Write an email giving advice. Use the model and your ideas from Part A to help you.

C Group work Share your emails. Do you agree with the advice? What other advice can you give? Discuss your ideas.

> Dear T. J.,
> I read your email, and I understand your problem. It <u>is</u> possible to be jealous of a cat! I think it's important to find things that you can do with your friend and Peaches. It's a good idea to . . .

4 **Speaking** Take it or leave it.

A Imagine you have two relationship problems. Write two sentences about each one. Be creative!

B Group work Share your imaginary problems. Your group gives advice. Take turns.

> 1. My friends never remember my birthday. I always remember theirs!
> 2. My parents don't trust me. I need to call them every three hours.

A: *I have a problem. My friends never remember my birthday. I always remember theirs!*
B: *It's a good idea to help them remember. Why not send them reminders?*

C Group work Whose advice do you think you'd follow? Why? Tell your group.

I can give advice about relationships. ☑

Wrap-up

1 Quick pair review

Lesson A **Brainstorm!** Make a list of tips for healthy family relationships. How many can you think of? You have five minutes.

Lesson B **Test your partner!** Apologize to your partner for three different things. Can your partner accept your apologies in three different ways? Take turns. You have two minutes.

Lesson C **Guess!** Speculate about a celebrity, but don't say his or her name! Can your partner guess who it is? Take turns. You have two minutes.

A: *This person might win an award for his new movie.*
B: *Is it . . . ?*

Lesson D **Find out!** What is the best relationship advice your partner has ever received? Who gave the advice? You have two minutes.

2 In the real world

What advice do the experts give? Go online and find advice in English about one of these topics. Then write about it.

a jealous friend	a neighbor's noisy dog
a friend who talks too much	an annoying boss
a lazy husband or wife	an inconsiderate neighbor

Dealing with Jealous Friends
I found a website that gives advice about jealous friends. If you have a jealous friend, try to find out why the friend is jealous. Try to understand how your friend feels. It's a good idea to tell your friend about a time when you felt jealous, too. That way she will not feel alone or embarrassed. Tell your friend what you did to feel better. Another piece of advice on the website is . . .

Living your life

LESSON **A**	LESSON **B**	LESSON **C**	LESSON **D**
• Qualities for success	• Advising against something	• Separable phrasal verbs	• Reading: "A Walk Across Japan"
• Reflexive pronouns	• Considering advice	• Second conditional	• Writing: An accomplishment

Warm-up

Realizado, Finalizado

A Look at the pictures. What have the people accomplished?

B What are some of your accomplishments? What other things would you like to accomplish in your life?

A He taught himself.

1 Vocabulary Qualities for success

A 🔊 Match the words and their meanings. Then listen and check your answers.

1. bravery _____   a. the ability to develop original ideas
2. confidence _____   b. the belief that you can succeed
3. creativity _____   c. a commitment to something
4. dedication _____   d. the quality of showing no fear

5. enthusiasm _____   e. the ability to change easily
6. flexibility _____   f. a strong interest in something
7. talent _____   g. the ability to make good decisions
8. wisdom _____   h. the natural ability to do things well

B 🔊 Complete the chart with the correct adjective forms for the nouns. Then listen and check your answers.

Noun	Adjective		Noun	Adjective
bravery	*brave*		enthusiasm	
confidence			flexibility	
creativity			talent	
dedication			wisdom	

C **Pair work** Which qualities in Part A do you think people are born with? Which do they develop from experience or by watching others? Discuss your ideas.

2 Language in context A success story

A 🔊 Read the story of Yong-eun Yang. What did he do in 2009?

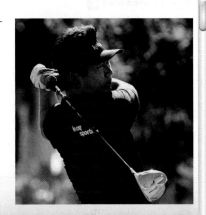

○ ○ ○

WEB ENCYCLOPEDIA

Yong-eun Yang

In his late teens, South Korea's Yong-eun Yang, or "Y. E.," enjoyed lifting weights and hoped to own his own gym someday. But that dream died when he hurt himself in the gym. So at age 19, he took a part-time job at a golf course. He picked up golf balls and began to observe other players. He started to practice the game by himself late at night, and he even forced himself to get up early to be at the course by 5:00 a.m. for more practice. This is how Y. E. taught himself to play golf. His dedication and patience paid off. He became a professional golfer in 1995, and, in 2009, this talented man won his first championship, beating Tiger Woods.

B What other qualities for success do you think Y. E. has?

3 Grammar 🔊 Reflexive pronouns

Use reflexive pronouns when the subject and object of a sentence refer to the same person or thing.

I hurt **myself** at work.
He taught **himself** to play golf.
They consider **themselves** brave.

By with a reflexive pronoun means "alone."
She traveled **by herself** to the United States.
Do you like to practice with another person or **by yourself**?

Personal pronouns	Reflexive pronouns
I	myself
you	yourself
he	himself
she	herself
it	itself
we	ourselves
you	yourselves
they	themselves

Complete the sentences with the correct reflexive pronouns. Then compare with a partner.

1. I drew a picture of _____ in art class.
2. I like your new hairstyle. Did you cut it _____ ?
3. If you and Joe have problems, you need to help _____ .
4. They had a great time. They really enjoyed _____ .
5. My brother doesn't consider _____ brave, but he is.
6. Heather wrote that by _____ . Nobody helped her.
7. We taught _____ Spanish before we moved to Peru.
8. I hurt _____ at the gym last week. My arm still hurts.
9. I took a trip by _____ . It helped me be more confident.

4 Pronunciation Stress shifts

🔊 Listen and repeat. Notice the stress shifts when some words change from nouns to adjectives.

crea**ti**vity	dedi**ca**tion	en**thu**siasm	flexi**bi**lity
crea**ti**ve	**de**dicated	enthusi**a**stic	**flex**ible

5 Speaking Self talk

A Pair work Interview your partner. Ask questions for more information. Take notes.

- Have you ever hurt yourself?
- Do you consider yourself brave?
- Have you ever traveled by yourself?
- Have you ever taught yourself something?
- Are you enjoying yourself in this class?
- Do you consider yourself a flexible person?

B Pair work Tell another classmate about your partner.

"William hurt himself once. He broke his foot."

6 Keep talking!

Go to page 144 for more practice.

I can talk about myself and my experiences. ☑

B I'll give it some thought.

1 Interactions   Giving and considering advice

A What do you do if you have too much work or studying to do?
Do you talk to anyone?

B 🔊 Listen to the conversation. What is Bryan thinking about doing?
Then practice the conversation.

Marta: What's wrong, Bryan?
Bryan: Well, my job is just really stressful right now. My boss just seems to give me more and more work. It's not fair.
Marta: That's not good.
Bryan: Actually, I'm thinking about quitting and looking for another job.
Marta: Really? I wouldn't recommend that.
Bryan: Why not?
Marta: Well, because you may not find something better. And that would just give you more stress. Have you thought about talking to your boss?
Bryan: Not really.
Marta: Why don't you try that? Maybe there is something he can do.
Bryan: I'll see.

C 🔊 Read the expressions below. Complete each box with a similar expression from the conversation. Then listen and check your answers.

Advising against something	*Considering advice*
_____	_____
I don't think you should do that.	I'll think about it.
I'm not sure that's the best idea.	I'll give it some thought.

D How would you respond? Write A (advise against it) or C (consider it). Then practice with a partner.

1. I think you should call the doctor. _____
2. I plan to study all night before my test. _____
3. I recommend that you stay home tomorrow if you don't feel well. _____
4. I think you should visit your grandmother this weekend. _____
5. I'm going to paint my house bright pink. _____
6. I'm not going to class tomorrow because I want to watch a soccer game. _____

2 **Listening** Maybe I'll do that.

A 🔊 Listen to Tim give advice to three friends. What is each friend's problem?
Check (✓) the correct answers.

Problems	Recommendations
1. ☐ She needs to get a full-time job. ☐ She wants to take more classes. ☐ She's thinking about quitting her job. ☐ She's not going to graduate.	
2. ☐ He doesn't have the money. ☐ He doesn't have a credit card. ☐ The leather jacket doesn't fit. ☐ His friend won't lend him any money.	
3. ☐ She takes too many breaks. ☐ She can't do a math problem. ☐ She drank too much coffee. ☐ Tim is driving her crazy.	

B 🔊 Listen again. What does Tim tell each friend to do? Complete the chart with
his recommendations.

3 **Speaking** Think about it!

A Imagine your friend wants to do the things below. What advice would you give?
Write notes.

- Your friend wants to buy a new, expensive
car. He doesn't have the money, and he
doesn't know how to drive!

- Your friend wants to take two more
classes. He's already taking five classes,
and he has a part-time job!

- Your friend wants to go camping in the
mountains by himself for a week. He's
never gone camping before!

B Pair work Role-play the situations in Part A. Then change roles.

Student A: Imagine you want to do the things in Part A. Tell Student B what you want
to do and why. Consider his or her advice.

Student B: Advise Student A against doing the things in Part A and explain why.
Recommend something else. Use your ideas from Part A.

A: *I saw this really awesome car yesterday! I think I'm going to buy it.*
B: *I'm not sure that's the best idea.*
A: *Why not?*

> I can *advise against something.* ☑
> I can *consider advice.* ☑

C What would you do?

1 Vocabulary Separable phrasal verbs

A 🔊 Match the phrasal verbs and their meanings. Then listen and check your answers.

1. He won't talk about his job, so don't **bring** it **up**. _____	a. donate
2. I got a bad grade on this essay. I need to **do** it **over**. _____	b. return money
3. I don't need these books. I might **give** them **away**. _____	c. mention
4. This is Lynn's camera. I need to **give** it **back**. _____	d. do again
5. Paul lent me some money. I need to **pay** him **back**. _____	e. return

6. Which one is Susan? Can you **point** her **out**? _____	f. do later
7. We can't have this meeting now. Let's **put** it **off**. _____	g. identify
8. This is serious. We need to **talk** it **over**. _____	h. not accept
9. I may buy that car, but I want to **try** it **out** first. _____	i. use
10. I have a job offer, but I plan to **turn** it **down**. _____	j. discuss

B Pair work What have you done over, talked over, paid back, tried out, or put off recently? Tell your partner.

A: *Have you done anything over recently?*
B: *Yes, I have. I did my English homework over last night. I made a lot of mistakes the first time!*

2 Conversation I'm kind of broke.

A 🔊 Listen to the conversation. What is Neil thinking about doing?

Dana: I really like your camcorder.
Neil: Actually, it's my friend Ben's. I'm just trying it out this week. I need to give it back to him tomorrow.
Dana: It looks really expensive.
Neil: It is. I'm thinking about buying one, but I can't right now.
Dana: Why not?
Neil: Well, I'm kind of broke. If I had more money, I'd buy it.
Dana: It would be nice to be rich, wouldn't it?
Neil: Tell me about it. What would you do if you were rich?
Dana: Hmm. . . . If I were rich, I'd travel. I'd give some money away, too.
Neil: That's nice.

B 🔊 Listen to the rest of the conversation. Why does Neil want a camcorder?

3 Grammar ◀)) Second conditional

Second conditional sentences describe "unreal" or imaginary situations. Use a past tense verb in the if *clause (the condition). Use* would *in the main clause.*

What **would** you **do** if you **had** more money?

    If I **had** more money, I **would buy** a camcorder.

Use were *for the past tense of* be *in the condition.*

Would you **travel** if you **were** rich?

    Yes, I **would**.   No, I **wouldn't**.

    Yes. If I **were** rich, I**'d travel** a lot.   No. I **wouldn't travel** a lot if I **were** rich.

A Complete the conversations with the correct words. Then compare with a partner.

1. **A:** What _____ you _____ (do) if you suddenly _____ (become) rich?

   B: I _____ (quit) my job. Then I _____ (travel) for a few months.

2. **A:** If a teacher _____ (give) you a good grade by mistake, what _____ you _____ (do)?

   B: I _____ (not / feel) right about it. I _____ (point) out the mistake.

3. **A:** How _____ you _____ (feel) if a friend _____ (call) you late at night?

   B: I _____ (be) surprised, but I _____ (not / feel) angry.

4. **A:** If you _____ (have) a relationship problem, who _____ you _____ (talk) to?

   B: I _____ (talk) about the problem with my best friend.

B Pair work Ask and answer the questions in Part A. Answer with your own information.

4 Speaking What would you do?

A Pair work Discuss the questions. Take notes.

- Where would you go if you had a lot of money?
- What would you give away if you were rich?
- What would you do if you saw your teacher or your boss at the supermarket?
- When would you turn down a job offer?
- Would you point out a mistake if a classmate made one? Why or why not?
- What would you do over if you had the chance?

B Group work Share your ideas with another pair. Are your ideas similar or different?

5 Keep talking!

Go to page 145 for more practice.

I can talk about imaginary situations. ✓

D What an accomplishment!

1 Reading

A What do you think it would be like to walk across your country? Why?

B Read the interview. Why did Mary and Etsuko often have to walk between 30 and 40 kilometers a day?

A Walk Across Japan

Mary King and Etsuko Shimabukuro completed a 7,974-kilometer walk across Japan. Mary takes our questions about their incredible accomplishment.

Why did you walk across Japan?
The mapmaker Ino Tadataka *inspired* me. He spent 17 years *on and off* walking through Japan. He drew the country's first real maps.

How long did it take?
A year and a half. We walked from the island of Hokkaido, in the north, down to Okinawa. In Hokkaido, we walked about 40 kilometers a day, and on the other islands, about 30. We often had no choice about the distance because we had to find a place to sleep.

Describe a typical day.
There really wasn't one, but we tried to start by 7:00 a.m. and walk for 10 to 12 hours. Sometimes we had breakfast on the road. We had to be careful in Hokkaido because the bears there could smell our food. We saw bears twice, which was terrifying!

Did you walk every day?
No. We needed to do our laundry, check our email, and rest. Also, I wanted to interview people for my blog.

What were some of the best parts?
There were many! We stayed in a *haunted* guesthouse, walked on fire at a festival, and visited many wonderful hot springs.

Any low points?
You know, overall, we really enjoyed ourselves, but there were a lot of aches and pains along the way. The traffic could be scary because there weren't always sidewalks for *pedestrians*.

Did you ever think about *giving up*?
No, we never wanted to stop. Actually, I was sad when it ended. I wanted to walk from Okinawa back to Tokyo, but Etsuko said we had to accept that we accomplished our goal. It was time to go home.

Would you do it over again?
Definitely. I'd love to *retrace* our steps when I'm 80. But I've also set myself the goal of walking across the U.K. or India someday.

Source: http://japanonfoot.blogspot.com

C Find the words in *italics* in the article. What do they mean? Write the words next to the correct definitions.

1. inhabited by ghosts ___*haunted*___
2. quitting _____
3. people who walk _____
4. go back over a route again _____
5. with breaks _____
6. gave someone an idea _____

D Pair work How would you describe Mary's personality? Do you know anyone like her?

2 Listening Can I ask you . . . ?

A Listen to four people talk about their biggest accomplishments this year. Write the accomplishments in the chart.

	Accomplishments	Qualities for success
1.		
2.		
3.		
4.		

B Listen again. What quality led to each person's success? Complete the chart.

C Pair work Who do you think had the biggest accomplishment? Why? Discuss your ideas.

3 Writing An accomplishment

A Write a paragraph about something you accomplished in your lifetime. Use the questions and the model to help you.

- What did you accomplish?
- Why did you decide to do it?
- How did you accomplish it?
- What was challenging about it?
- Why was it important?

B Group work Share your paragraphs. How are your accomplishments similar or different?

A Healthy Change
I decided that I wanted to change something at our school. A lot of the vending machines had very unhealthy food, like chocolate, candy, and potato chips. Students wanted healthier food like fruits and yogurt. So I asked students and teachers to sign a petition to get healthier food. It was difficult at first . . .

4 Speaking What have you done?

Class activity Find people who have done these things. Write their names and ask questions for more information.

Find someone who has . . .	Name	Extra information
helped someone with a challenging task		
won an award for doing something		
learned a new skill outside of school		
solved a problem at school, home, or work		
used technology to improve his or her English		

I can ask and talk about accomplishments.

Wrap-up

1 Quick pair review

Lesson A **Test your partner!** Say three personal pronouns. Can your partner use the correct reflexive pronouns in sentences? Take turns. You have two minutes.

A: *He.*
B: *Himself. My neighbor introduced himself to me yesterday.*

Lesson B **Do you remember?** Which sentences are advising against something? Check (✓) the correct answers. You have one minute.

- ☐ I don't think you should do that.
- ☐ Please don't worry about it.
- ☐ I'm not sure that's the best idea.
- ☐ I'll give it some thought.
- ☐ I'd rather not answer that.
- ☐ I wouldn't recommend that.

Lesson C **Find out!** What is one thing both you and your partner would do in each situation? You have three minutes.

- Where would you go if you won a free vacation?
- What would you buy if you received money for your birthday?
- What would you do if you lost your cell phone?

Lesson D **Brainstorm!** Make a list of accomplishments. How many can you think of? You have two minutes.

2 In the real world

Which country would you like to travel across? Go online and find information in English about one of these trips or your own idea. Then answer the questions and write about it.

a car trip across the United States	a train trip across Canada
a bike trip across France	a walking trip across England

- How far is it?
- How long would it take?
- How much would it cost?
- What would you need to take?
- Where would you stay?

> *A Road Trip in the U.S.A.*
> *I'd take a car trip across the United States. I'd start in Ocean City, Maryland, and drive to San Francisco, California. The trip is about 3,000 miles. The first place I would stop is . . .*

Music

LESSON A	LESSON B	LESSON C	LESSON D
• Compound adjectives • Past passive	• Giving instructions	• Verb and noun formation • Present perfect with *yet* and *already*	• Reading: "Richie Starr" • Writing: A music review

Warm-up

Music Sales in the U.S.A.

other* 16%
jazz 1%
classical 2%
gospel 7%
pop 9%
R & B 10%
hip-hop 11%
rock 32%
country 12%

* Includes new age, soundtracks, electronic, ethnic, folk, etc.

Source: The Recording Industry Association of America, 2008

A Label the pictures with the correct types of music from the chart.

B What do you think are the most popular kinds of music where you live? What's your favorite kind of music? What's your least favorite? Why?

A Music trivia

1 Vocabulary Compound adjectives

A 🔊 Complete the compound adjectives with the correct participles.
Then listen and check your answers.

Compound adjective		Present participle
award-_**winning**_	video	selling
best-_____	artist	winning ✓
nice-_____	voice	breaking
record-_____	hit	sounding

Compound adjective		Past participle
high-_____	ticket	downloaded
oddly _____	group	priced
often-_____	performer	named
well-_____	singer	known

B **Pair work** Ask and answer questions with each phrase in Part A.
Answer with your own ideas.

> **A:** *Can you name an award-winning video?*
> **B:** *Yes. Michael Jackson's video for "Thriller" won a lot of awards.*

2 Language in context Musical firsts

A 🔊 Read about these musical firsts. Which were downloaded?

Milestones in Music History

The first rap recording was made by the Sugarhill Gang. In 1979, the band's song "Rapper's Delight" became the first rap song to make the U.S. pop charts.

The song "Crazy" by Gnarls Barkley was leaked in 2005, months before its release. When it was finally released in March 2006, it became the first song to reach number one from downloaded sales.

The band Radiohead was the first to sell their album online for whatever people wanted to pay. Over a million albums were downloaded before the CD was released in December 2007.

The well-known band Aerosmith was the first to have a video game created around their music. People can play the guitar and sing along to 41 of their songs. The game was released in June 2008.

B What else do you know about these musical firsts? Do you know of any others?

"The band Run-DMC also recorded the song 'Rapper's Delight.'"

104

3 Grammar 🔊 **Past passive**

The passive voice places the focus of a sentence on the receiver of an action instead of the doer of the action.

Active voice (simple past)
Fans **downloaded** <u>over a million albums</u>.

Passive voice (past of be *+ past participle)*
<u>Over a million albums</u> **were downloaded**.

Use the passive voice when the doer of the action is not known or not important.
The game **was released** in 2008.

When the doer of the action is important to know, use the passive voice with by.
The first rap recording **was made** <u>by</u> the Sugarhill Gang.

A Complete the sentences with the past passive forms of the verbs.
Then compare with a partner.

1. All of the high-priced tickets to the concert _____ (sell) online.
2. The best-selling artists of the year _____ (give) a special award.
3. The singer's record-breaking hit _____ (write) by her mother.
4. The performer's biggest hit song _____ (use) in a TV commercial.
5. The band's award-winning video _____ (see) by millions of people.
6. The songs on her album _____ (play) with traditional instruments.

B Pair work Say the trivia about the music group the Beatles.
Your partner changes the sentences to use the past passive. Take turns.

1. In 1960, John Lennon suggested the name "the Beatles."
2. Ringo Starr replaced the original drummer, Peter Best, in 1962.
3. Paul McCartney wrote "Hey Jude" for John Lennon's son Julian.
4. Many people called George Harrison "the quiet Beatle."
5. *Rolling Stone* magazine chose the Beatles as the best artists of all time.

A: *In 1960, John Lennon suggested the name "the Beatles."*
B: *In 1960, the name "the Beatles" was suggested by John Lennon.*

4 Speaking Name it!

A Write three sentences in the past passive about the same song, singer, musician, band, or album, but don't use the name!

B Group work Share your sentences. Your group guesses the name of the song, singer, musician, band, or album. Take turns.

1. *This singer's first album was called* The Fame.
2. *She was born in New York City.*
3. *She was made famous by her music and fashion statements.*
(*answer: Lady Gaga*)

5 Keep talking!

Go to page **146** for more practice.

I can *talk about music.* ☑

1 Interactions   Giving instructions

A What kinds of things do you use a computer for? How did you learn to do those things?

B 🔊 Listen to the conversation. What steps does Roger follow to download and play a song? Then practice the conversation.

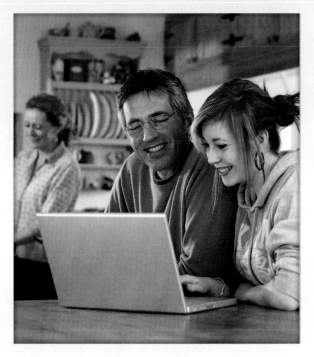

Roger: This is so frustrating!

Dena: What are you doing, Dad?

Roger: I'm trying to download a song, but I'm not having much luck. What am I doing wrong?

Dena: It's not that hard. Here, let me show you.

Roger: Thanks.

Dena: First, type in the name of the artist or the title of the song in this search box and hit "search."

Roger: OK. Ah, here we go.

Dena: Next, choose the song you want and click "download."

Roger: Oh, look at that. It's so fast! Is that it?

Dena: Well, no. Finally, click "play."

C 🔊 Read the expressions below. Complete each box with a similar expression from the conversation. Then listen and check your answers.

Beginning instructions	*Continuing instructions*	*Ending instructions*
_____	_____	_____
To start, . . .	Then . . .	To finish, . . .
The first thing you do is . . .	After that, . . .	The last thing you do is . . .

D Pair work Number the instructions from 1 to 5. Then have a conversation like the one in Part B.

How to download a ringtone:

_____ Select the ringtone that you want.

_____ Register with the site that you chose.

_____ Send the ringtone to your phone by text.

_____ Listen to the ringtones that are available.

_____ Find websites that offer ringtones.

2 Listening How does it work?

A 🔊 Listen to people give instructions on how to use three different machines. Number the machines from 1 to 3. There is one extra machine.

B 🔊 Listen again. Each person makes one mistake when giving instructions. Write the mistakes.

1. She said _____ instead of _____ .
2. He said _____ instead of _____ .
3. She said _____ instead of _____ .

C Pair work Choose one of the machines above, and give instructions on how to use it. Add any additional instructions.

"To use a record player, first plug it in. Then . . ."

3 Speaking Step-by-step

A Pair work Choose a topic from the list below or your own idea. Make a list of instructions about how to do it.

attach a file to an email	*How to* _____
burn a CD or DVD	*1.*
create a playlist	*2.*
download a podcast	
make an international call	*3.*
send a text message	*4.*
upload a video	*5.*

B Pair work Give your instructions to another classmate. Answer any questions.

A: *To attach a file to an email, first open your email account.*
   After that, click "compose." Next, . . .

I can give instructions. ☑

C Music and me

1 Vocabulary Verb and noun formation

A 🔊 Match the phrases and the pictures. Then listen and check your answers.

a. **announce** a tour	c. **compose** music	e. **perform** a song	g. **record** a song
b. **appreciate** music	d. **entertain** an audience	f. **produce** a song	h. **release** a new album

 1. ☐
 2. ☐
 3. ☐
 4. ☐

 5. ☐
 6. ☐
 7. ☐
 8. ☐

B 🔊 Write the noun forms of the verbs in Part A. Then listen and check your answers.

a. ___*announcement*___   c. _____   e. _____   g. _____

b. _____   d. _____   f. _____   h. _____

C Pair work Do you know any friends, artists, or other people who do or have done the things in Part A? Tell your partner.

2 Conversation I'm his biggest fan!

A 🔊 Listen to the conversation. What does Andy tell Miranda to listen to?

Andy: Oh, look! Richie Starr is going to perform here.

Miranda: Yeah, I know. I'm planning to go.

Andy: Really? Have you gotten a ticket yet?

Miranda: Not yet. But I think you can still get them. I didn't know you were a fan.

Andy: Are you kidding? I'm his biggest fan!

Miranda: Have you heard his new album?

Andy: He hasn't released it yet. But I've already downloaded his new single. Here, listen.

Miranda: Nice! I hear he has a cool online fan club.

Andy: He does. It gives information about new album releases and announces all upcoming performances.

B 🔊 Listen to the rest of the conversation. Why didn't Andy know about the concert?

3 Grammar ◀)) Present perfect with *yet* and *already*

In questions, use *yet when you expect the action to have happened.*	In responses, already *means the action has happened earlier.*	In responses, yet *means the action hasn't happened, but you expect it to.*
Have you **gotten** a ticket **yet**?	Yes, I**'ve already gotten** a ticket.	No, I **haven't gotten** a ticket **yet**.
Has he **released** his album **yet**?	Yes, he**'s already released** it.	No, **not yet**. He **hasn't released** it **yet**.

A Write sentences in the present perfect with *already* and *yet* about Richie Starr's goals. Then compare with a partner.

1. *Richie has already written four new songs.*
2. _____
3. _____
4. _____
5. _____
6. _____

Richie Starr's Goals
✓ *write four new songs*
  record two songs for his album
  release his new album
✓ *entertain children at the hospital*
✓ *give a free performance in the park*
  announce his retirement

B Pair work Look at Richie's list in Part A. Ask questions with *yet* and answer them.

4 Pronunciation Syllable stress

A ◀)) Listen and repeat. Notice how the stress stays on the same syllable when these verbs become nouns.

an**nounce**	enter**tain**	per**form**	pro**duce**
an**nounce**ment	enter**tain**ment	per**form**ance	pro**duc**tion

B ◀)) Listen. Circle the verb-noun pairs if the stress stays the same.

appreciate	compose	record	release
appreciation	composition	recording	release

5 Speaking The latest

A Class activity Complete the questions with your own ideas. Then find someone who has already done each thing, and ask questions for more information.

• Have you heard _____ (a new album or song) yet?
• Have you played _____ (a new video game) yet?
• Have you seen _____ (a new TV show or movie) yet?
• _____ ?

B Group work Share your information.

6 Keep talking!

Student A go to page **147** and
Student B go to page **148** for more practice.

I can talk about things I've done recently. ☑

D *Thoughts on music*

1 Reading 🔊

A What are "fan sites"? Who usually has them? What kind of information do the websites usually include?

B Look at the fan site. What things can fans do on this site?

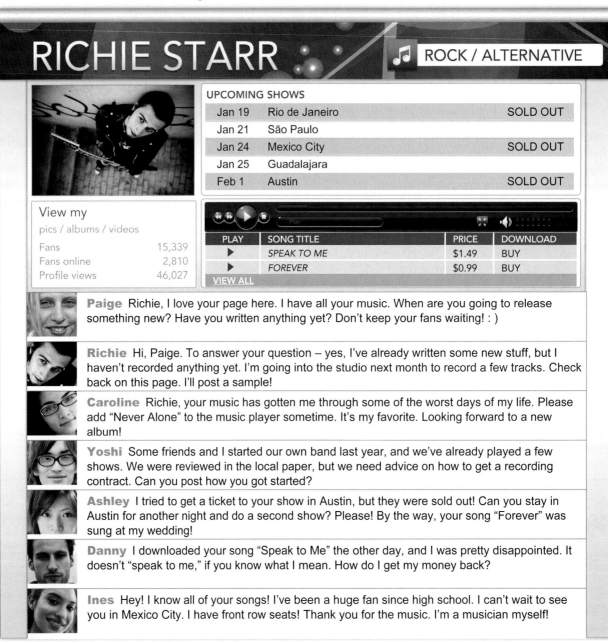

RICHIE STARR 🎵 ROCK / ALTERNATIVE

UPCOMING SHOWS

Jan 19	Rio de Janeiro	SOLD OUT
Jan 21	São Paulo	
Jan 24	Mexico City	SOLD OUT
Jan 25	Guadalajara	
Feb 1	Austin	SOLD OUT

View my
pics / albums / videos

Fans	15,339
Fans online	2,810
Profile views	46,027

PLAY	SONG TITLE	PRICE	DOWNLOAD
▶	*SPEAK TO ME*	$1.49	BUY
▶	*FOREVER*	$0.99	BUY
VIEW ALL			

Paige Richie, I love your page here. I have all your music. When are you going to release something new? Have you written anything yet? Don't keep your fans waiting! :)

Richie Hi, Paige. To answer your question – yes, I've already written some new stuff, but I haven't recorded anything yet. I'm going into the studio next month to record a few tracks. Check back on this page. I'll post a sample!

Caroline Richie, your music has gotten me through some of the worst days of my life. Please add "Never Alone" to the music player sometime. It's my favorite. Looking forward to a new album!

Yoshi Some friends and I started our own band last year, and we've already played a few shows. We were reviewed in the local paper, but we need advice on how to get a recording contract. Can you post how you got started?

Ashley I tried to get a ticket to your show in Austin, but they were sold out! Can you stay in Austin for another night and do a second show? Please! By the way, your song "Forever" was sung at my wedding!

Danny I downloaded your song "Speak to Me" the other day, and I was pretty disappointed. It doesn't "speak to me," if you know what I mean. How do I get my money back?

Ines Hey! I know all of your songs! I've been a huge fan since high school. I can't wait to see you in Mexico City. I have front row seats! Thank you for the music. I'm a musician myself!

C Read the fan site. Answer the questions.

1. Who has concert tickets? _____
2. Who can't get concert tickets? _____
3. Who wants advice? _____
4. Who is unhappy with a song? _____
5. Who has Richie's music helped? _____
6. Who has all of Richie's music? _____

D Pair work Do you ever look at fan sites of musicians, actors, or athletes? Why or why not? Tell your partner.

2 **Writing** A music review

A Write a review of an album (or a song) you'd recommend. Use the questions and the model to help you.

- What's the name of the album / song?
- When was it released?
- What do you like about the album / song?
- Is there anything you don't like about it?
- Why would you recommend it?

B **Class activity** Post your reviews around the room. Read your classmates' reviews. Which songs or albums have you heard?

Momento

Bebel Gilberto's album Momento was released in 2007. All of the songs are good, but the title song is excellent. On the album, she blends Brazilian bossa nova with electronica and has a beautiful-sounding voice. The only thing I don't like about it is that there aren't enough songs! I'd recommend it because it was recorded with Japanese guitarist Masa Shimizu and . . .

3 **Listening** Song dedications

A 🔊 Listen to five people call a radio show to dedicate songs to their friends and family members. Who do they dedicate songs to? Write the people in the chart.

	People	Song titles
1.	friend	
2.		
3.		
4.		
5.		

B 🔊 Listen again. What are the song titles? Complete the chart.

C **Pair work** Imagine you can dedicate a song to someone. What song would you dedicate and to whom? Why? Tell your partner.

4 **Speaking** Soundtrack of my life

A Make a list of three songs that remind you of particular times or events in your life.

	Song titles	Memories
1.		
2.		
3.		

B **Group work** Discuss your songs and memories. Ask and answer questions for more information.

A: *The song . . . reminds me of middle school. It was my favorite song when I was 14.*
B: *I know that song! How do you feel now when you hear it?*
A: *Oh, I feel totally embarrassed. I can't stand it now!*

> *I can talk about memorable songs.* ✓

Wrap-up

1 Quick pair review

Lesson A Brainstorm! Make a list of words and phrases related to music.
How many do you know? You have two minutes.

Lesson B Do you remember? Complete the sentences with words or phrases
to give instructions. You have one minute.

How to install software:

_____ turn on your computer.

_____ insert the CD and click "install."

_____ to do is restart your computer.

How to get money out of an ATM:

_____ put your ATM card in the machine.

_____ type in your code.

_____ select how much money you want.

Lesson C Find out! What are two things both you and your partner have
already done today? What are two things you both haven't done yet? You have
three minutes.

Lesson D Test your partner! Say (or sing) the words to a song you know
in English. Can your partner guess the title and singer? You have two minutes.

2 In the real world

Who is your favorite singer? Go to the singer's website, and find information
about his or her albums. Then write about them.

- What was the singer's first album? When was it released?
- When was the singer's last album released? Did it have any hit songs?
- What's your favorite song by this singer? What's it about?

> *Taylor Swift*
> My favorite singer is Taylor Swift. Her first album
> was called Taylor Swift. It was released in 2006.
> I love it. My favorite song on the album is called "Tim
> McGraw", who is a famous country music singer
> himself. Taylor was only sixteen years old when the
> song was released. The song is about how one of Tim
> McGraw's songs always reminds her of . . .

On vacation

LESSON **A**	LESSON **B**	LESSON **C**	LESSON **D**
• Vacation activities • Gerunds	• Asking about preferences • Reminding someone of something	• Extreme sports • Modals for necessity and recommendations	• Reading: "A Taste of Cairo" • Writing: A walking tour

Warm-up

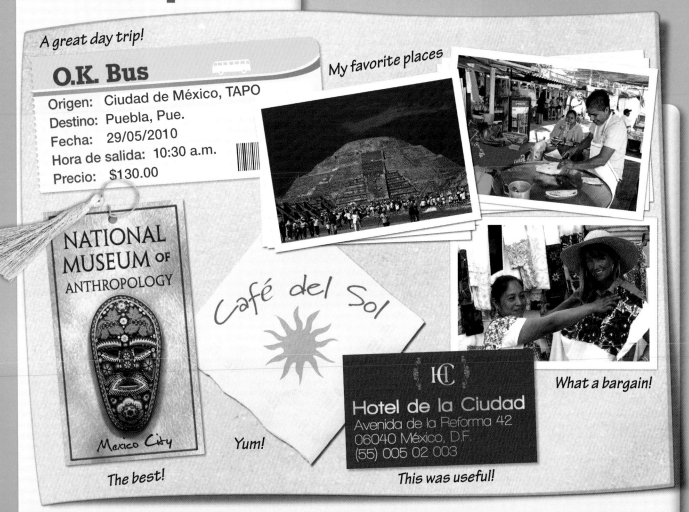

A great day trip!

O.K. Bus

Origen: Ciudad de México, TAPO
Destino: Puebla, Pue.
Fecha: 29/05/2010
Hora de salida: 10:30 a.m.
Precio: $130.00

NATIONAL MUSEUM OF ANTHROPOLOGY

Mexico City

The best!

Café del Sol

Yum!

My favorite places

Hotel de la Ciudad
Avenida de la Reforma 42
06040 México, D.F.
(55) 005 02 003

This was useful!

What a bargain!

A Look at Julie's scrapbook. Where did she go on her vacation? What do you think she did there?

B What do you like to do on vacation? What kinds of things do you usually bring back with you?

A Travel preferences

1 Vocabulary Vacation activities

A 🔊 Match the phrases and the pictures. Then listen and check your answers.

a. buy handicrafts	c. listen to live music	e. speak a foreign language	g. visit landmarks
b. go to clubs	d. see wildlife	f. try local food	h. volunteer

1. ☐

2. ☐

3. ☐

4. ☐

5. ☐

6. ☐

7. ☐

8. ☐

B Pair work Which things in Part A have you *never* done on vacation?
Tell your partner.

2 Language in context Three types of tours

A 🔊 Read the ads for three tours. Which tour is best for someone who
likes volunteering? someone who likes eating? someone who dislikes planning?

Cuisine Adventures

Trying local foods is a great
way to learn about a culture.
Call today if you are interested
in joining our "Eat and Learn"
tour.

ENVIRONMENTAL EXPERIENCES

Are you concerned about
protecting the environment?
Volunteering is a rewarding
way to spend a vacation.
Choose from over 20 tours.

No Worries Tours

Do you enjoy traveling by
bus but dislike planning the
details? We specialize in
organizing tours with no
stress.

B What about you? Which tour interests you? Why?

3 Grammar 🔊 Gerunds

A gerund is an -ing word that acts like a noun. Gerunds may be the subject
of a sentence, or they may appear after some verbs or prepositions.

As subjects:	**Trying** local foods is a great way to learn about a culture.
	Volunteering is a rewarding way to spend a vacation.
After some verbs:	I **enjoy traveling** by bus.
	I **dislike planning** the travel details.
After prepositions:	I'm interested **in joining** the "Eat and Learn" tour.
	I'm concerned **about protecting** the environment.

A Complete the conversations with the gerund forms of the verbs.
Then compare with a partner.

be	buy	get	go	help	lose	meet	✓travel	try	volunteer

1. **A:** Do you enjoy ___*traveling*___ alone or in a group?

   B: I prefer _____ in a large group. It's more fun.

2. **A:** Are you interested in _____ handicrafts when you travel?

   B: Not really. I like _____ to markets, but just to look.

3. **A:** _____ local food is the best way to learn about a culture. Don't you agree?

   B: I'm not really sure. _____ local people is also good.

4. **A:** Are you worried about _____ sick when you travel abroad?

   B: Not really. I'm more concerned about _____ my passport!

5. **A:** Do you think _____ on vacation would be fun?

   B: I do. _____ other people is a great thing to do.

B Pair work Ask and answer the questions in Part A. Answer with your
own information.

4 Speaking Travel talk

A Complete the questions with your own ideas. Use gerunds.

- Do you enjoy _____ when you're on vacation?
- Are you interested in _____ on vacation?
- Which is more interesting on vacation, _____ or
  _____ ?
- Are you ever concerned about _____ when you travel?
- As a tourist, is _____ important to you?
- _____ ?
- _____ ?

B Group work Discuss your questions. Ask and answer questions
to get more information.

5 Keep talking!

Go to page 149 for more practice.

I can *discuss travel preferences.* ☑

1 Interactions Preferences and reminders

A Where do you usually stay when you travel? A hotel? A youth hostel?

B 🔊 Listen to the conversation. What doesn't the guest need help with?
Then practice the conversation.

Clerk: Can I help you?
Guest: Yes. I'm looking for a room for two nights.
Clerk: Do you have a reservation?
Guest: No, I don't.
Clerk: Let me see what we have. Would you like a single room or a double room?
Guest: A single is fine. I only need one bed.
Clerk: I can give you room 13A. Please sign here. And there's a free breakfast from 7:00 to 9:00.
Guest: Oh, great. Thank you very much.
Clerk: Here's your key. Do you need help with your bag?
Guest: No, that's all right.
Clerk: OK. Remember to leave your key at the front desk when you go out.
Guest: No problem.
Clerk: Enjoy your stay.

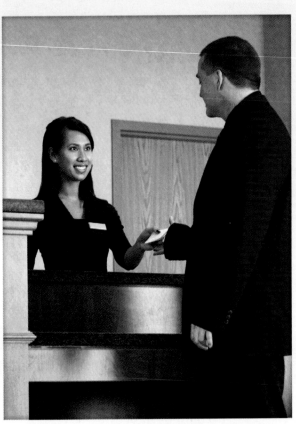

C 🔊 Read the expressions below. Complete each box with a similar expression from the conversation. Then listen and check your answers.

Asking about preferences
_____
Would you prefer . . . or . . . ?
Would you rather have . . . or . . . ?

Reminding someone of something
_____
Don't forget to . . .
Let me remind you to . . .

D Match the sentences and the responses. Then practice with a partner.

1. May I help you? _____
2. Would you like a single room? _____
3. Would you prefer a garden or an ocean view? _____
4. Please remember to lock your door at night. _____
5. Don't forget to check out by 11:00. _____

a. I don't know. Which one is cheaper?
b. Eleven? I thought it was by noon.
c. Actually, we need a double.
d. Yes. I have a reservation for one night.
e. I will. Thanks for the reminder.

2 **Listening** At a hostel

A 🔊 Listen to a backpacker check into a hostel. Complete the form with the correct information.

Sydney Backpackers

Type of room:

☐ single   ☐ double   ☐ triple   ☐ dorm

Number of nights? _____

Bathroom? ☐ yes ☐ no   **Breakfast?** ☐ yes ☐ no

Method of payment:

☐ cash   ☐ credit card

Room number: _____

B 🔊 Listen again. Answer the questions.

1. Why doesn't she get a single room? _____
2. What time is breakfast? _____
3. What floor is her room on? _____
4. What does the receptionist remind her to do? _____

3 **Speaking** Role play

Pair work Role-play the situation. Then change roles.

Student A: You want a room at a hotel. Student B is the clerk at the front desk. Circle your preferences. Then check in.

- You want a **single** / **double** room.
- You want to stay for **two** / **three** / **four** nights.
- You **want** / **don't want** your own bathroom.
- You **want** / **don't want** breakfast.

Student B: You are the clerk at the front desk of a hotel. Check Student A in. At the end, remind him or her of something.

B: *Can I help you?*
A: *Yes, thank you. I'd like a room, please.*
B: *All right. Would you prefer a single or a double?*
A: *I'd prefer . . .*
B: *How many nights would you like to stay?*
A: *. . .*
B: *. . . And please don't forget . . .*

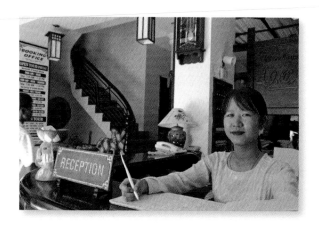

*I can **ask about preferences**.* ☑
*I can **remind someone of something**.* ☑

C Rules and recommendations

1 Vocabulary Extreme sports

A 🔊 Label the pictures with the correct words. Then listen and check your answers.

bungee jumping	paragliding	skydiving	waterskiing
kite surfing	rock climbing	snowboarding	white-water rafting

1. _____ 2. _____ 3. _____ 4. _____

5. _____ 6. _____ 7. _____ 8. _____

B Pair work Which sports would you consider trying? Which wouldn't you do? Why not? Tell your partner.

2 Conversation First-time snowboarder

A 🔊 Listen to the conversation. Why does Sarah tell Kyle to stay in the beginners' section?

Kyle: Hi. I'd like to rent a snowboard, please.

Sarah: OK. Have you ever been snowboarding?

Kyle: Um, no. But I've skied before.

Sarah: Well, we offer lessons. You don't have to take them, but it's a good idea. You'll learn the basics.

Kyle: All right. When is your next lesson?

Sarah: At 11:00. You've got to complete this form here to sign up.

Kyle: No problem. What else do I need to know?

Sarah: After your lesson, you should stay in the beginners' section for a while. It's safer for the other snowboarders.

Kyle: OK. Anything else?

Sarah: Yes. You must wear a helmet. Oh, and you ought to wear sunscreen. The sun can be very strong.

B 🔊 Listen to the conversation between Kyle and his instructor. Why is Kyle uncomfortable?

3 Grammar ◀)) Modals for necessity and recommendations

Necessity

You **must** wear a helmet.

You**'ve got to** complete this form.

You **have to** listen to your instructor.

Lack of necessity

You **don't have to** take a lesson.

Recommendations

You**'d better** be back before dark.

You **ought to** wear sunscreen.

You **should** stay in the beginners' section.

You **shouldn't** go in the advanced section.

A Circle the best travel advice. Then compare with a partner.

1. You **should / must** get a passport before you go abroad. Everybody needs one.
2. You **don't have to / 've got to** visit every landmark. Choose just a few instead.
3. You **should / don't have to** book a hotel online. It's often cheaper that way.
4. You **ought to / shouldn't** get to your hotel too early. You can't check in until 2:00.
5. You **shouldn't / 'd better** keep your money in a safe place. Losing it would be awful.
6. You **have to / should** pay for some things in cash. Many places don't take credit cards.
7. You **must / don't have to** show your student ID to get a discount. Don't forget it!
8. You **ought to / shouldn't** try some local food. It can be full of nice surprises!

B Pair work What advice would you give? Complete the sentences with modals for necessity or recommendations. Then compare answers.

1. You _____ go paragliding on a very windy day.
2. You _____ have experience to go waterskiing.
3. You _____ have special equipment to go bungee jumping.
4. You _____ be in good shape to go kite surfing.

4 Pronunciation Reduction of verbs

A ◀)) Listen and repeat. Notice the reduction of the modal verbs.

You've **got to** pay in cash.

You **have to** check out by noon.

You **ought to** try the food.

B Pair work Practice the sentences in Exercise 3. Reduce the modal verbs.

5 Speaking Rules of the game

A Group work Choose an extreme sport from Exercise 1. What rules do you think there are? What recommendations would you give to someone who wanted to try it?

A: *You must sign a form before you go bungee jumping.*
B: *Yeah. And you should wear a helmet.*
C: *Oh, and you shouldn't be afraid.*

B Class activity Share your ideas.

6 Keep talking!

Go to page 150 for more practice.

I can talk about rules and recommendations. ☑

D Seeing the sights

1 Reading 🔊

A Do you ever read food or travel blogs? Do you ever watch food or travel TV shows?

B Read the blog. Write the headings above the correct paragraphs.

> A Delicious Dinner   Juice Break   The Market   Sweet Shop

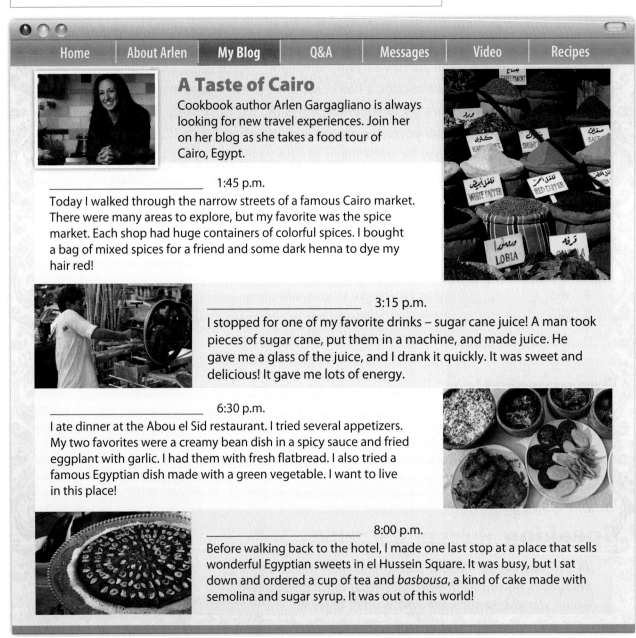

Home | About Arlen | **My Blog** | Q&A | Messages | Video | Recipes

A Taste of Cairo

Cookbook author Arlen Gargagliano is always looking for new travel experiences. Join her on her blog as she takes a food tour of Cairo, Egypt.

_____ 1:45 p.m.

Today I walked through the narrow streets of a famous Cairo market. There were many areas to explore, but my favorite was the spice market. Each shop had huge containers of colorful spices. I bought a bag of mixed spices for a friend and some dark henna to dye my hair red!

_____ 3:15 p.m.

I stopped for one of my favorite drinks – sugar cane juice! A man took pieces of sugar cane, put them in a machine, and made juice. He gave me a glass of the juice, and I drank it quickly. It was sweet and delicious! It gave me lots of energy.

_____ 6:30 p.m.

I ate dinner at the Abou el Sid restaurant. I tried several appetizers. My two favorites were a creamy bean dish in a spicy sauce and fried eggplant with garlic. I had them with fresh flatbread. I also tried a famous Egyptian dish made with a green vegetable. I want to live in this place!

_____ 8:00 p.m.

Before walking back to the hotel, I made one last stop at a place that sells wonderful Egyptian sweets in el Hussein Square. It was busy, but I sat down and ordered a cup of tea and *basbousa*, a kind of cake made with semolina and sugar syrup. It was out of this world!

C Read the blog again. Write the initials of the blog headings (D, J, M, or S) in which Arlen did the activities below. (More than one answer is possible.)

1. ate a meal _____   3. drank something _____   5. saw spices _____
2. bought a gift _____   4. had something sweet _____   6. tried vegetables _____

D Pair work Would you enjoy a tour like this? Why or why not? Discuss your ideas.

2 Writing A walking tour

A Pair work Choose a topic for an interesting walking tour in your town or city. Use one of the topics below or your own idea.

architecture and design	historical sights	parks and nature
food and drink	nightlife	shopping

B Pair work Write a description of your walking tour.

Historic Old San Juan

To really learn about the history of Puerto Rico, you have to walk through Old San Juan. You should start your walking tour at the city walls. Follow these walls along the sea to San Juan Gate, which was built around 1635. Go through the gate, turn right, and walk uphill. At the end of the street you can see La Fortaleza. . . .

C Group work Present your tour to another pair. Did you include any of the same places?

La Fortaleza
Old San Juan, Puerto Rico

3 Listening An adventure tour

A 🔊 Listen to a guide talk to some tourists before a Grand Canyon rafting trip. What does the guide tell the tourists to do? Check (✓) the correct answers.

- ☐ wear a safety vest
- ☐ drink a lot of water
- ☐ bring water
- ☐ bring food
- ☐ wear sunscreen
- ☐ wear a hat
- ☐ leave your camera
- ☐ bring plastic bags
- ☐ bring your cell phone
- ☐ wear a swimsuit
- ☐ wear tennis shoes
- ☐ listen to your guide

B 🔊 Listen again. Are the statements true or false? Write T (true) or F (false).

1. The most important thing to remember is to have fun. _____
2. The tourists need to wear safety vests at all times on the raft. _____
3. There is no eating or drinking allowed. _____
4. The tourists shouldn't leave their phones on the bus. _____

4 Speaking Dream trip

A Imagine you can go anywhere in the world for three weeks. Answer the questions.

- What kind of trip are you interested in taking?
- What places would you like to visit? Why?
- What would you like to do in each place?
- How long do you plan to spend in each place?
- How can you get from place to place?

B Pair work Tell your partner about your dream trip. Ask and answer questions for more information.

I can describe my dream trip.

Wrap-up

1 Quick pair review

Lesson A **Test your partner!** Say four vacation activities. Can your partner use the gerund form of the phrase in a sentence correctly? You have three minutes.

A: *See wildlife.*
B: *I'm not interested in seeing wildlife on vacation.*

Lesson B **Give your opinion!** Ask your partner which vacation he or she prefers from each pair of pictures. Then remind your partner to do or take something on the trip. Take turns. You have two minutes.

A: *Would you prefer going to an island or to the mountains?*
B: *I'd prefer going to an island.*
A: *OK. Remember to take sunscreen.*

Lesson C **Brainstorm!** Make a list of extreme sports people do in the water, in the air, and on land. How many do you know? You have one minute.

Lesson D **Guess!** Describe your dream trip to your partner, but don't say where it is. Can your partner guess where it is? Take turns. You have two minutes.

2 In the real world

Would you like to try a new sport? Go online and find recommendations in English for people who want to try a new sport. Use one of the sports below or your own idea. Then write about it.

sandboarding	downhill mountain biking	base jumping	bodyboarding

Sandboarding
Sandboarding is like snowboarding, but you do it on sand, not snow. You must have a sandboard for this sport. You should wear glasses so that you don't get sand in your eyes.

Left brain / right brain

A **Pair work** Interview your partner. Check (✓) his or her answers.

Left Brain **VS.** Right Brain

Do you use your right or left brain more often? Try this fun quiz and find out.

1. **How do you remember things?**
   - ☐ a. with words
   - ☐ b. with pictures
   - ☐ c. both

2. **Which can you remember easily?**
   - ☐ a. names
   - ☐ b. faces
   - ☐ c. both

3. **Which math subject do you like?**
   - ☐ a. algebra
   - ☐ b. geometry
   - ☐ c. both

4. **How do you like to work in class?**
   - ☐ a. alone
   - ☐ b. in groups
   - ☐ c. both

5. **How do you like to study alone?**
   - ☐ a. quietly
   - ☐ b. with music playing
   - ☐ c. both

6. **Which activity do you enjoy?**
   - ☐ a. writing
   - ☐ b. drawing
   - ☐ c. both

7. **What kinds of tests do you like?**
   - ☐ a. multiple choice
   - ☐ b. essay
   - ☐ c. both

8. **How do you like things explained to you?**
   - ☐ a. with words
   - ☐ b. with actions
   - ☐ c. both

9. **What do you use to make decisions?**
   - ☐ a. the facts
   - ☐ b. my experience
   - ☐ c. both

10. **How do you like to solve problems?**
    - ☐ a. one at a time
    - ☐ b. at the same time
    - ☐ c. both

11. **How do you manage your time?**
    - ☐ a. very carefully
    - ☐ b. not very carefully
    - ☐ c. both

12. **Which animals do you like?**
    - ☐ a. dogs
    - ☐ b. cats
    - ☐ c. both

Source: library.thinkquest.org

B **Pair work** Score your partner's answers. Is he or she left-brained or right-brained? (More *c* answers or the same number of *a* and *b* answers means your partner has traits for both.)

More *a* answers: Left-brained	**More *b* answers: Right-brained**
More verbal than visual	More visual than verbal
Likes to do things step by step	Likes to do things at the same time
Very organized	Not always organized
Follows rules without questioning	Often asks why
Strong sense of time	Little sense of time
Learns by seeing	Learns by doing
Uses few gestures when talking	Talks with hands
Listens to what is said	Listens to how something is said

C **Group work** Do your results in Part B describe you well? What do you think your results say about your personality?

People on my mind

A Write the name of someone you know for each description. Then think about answers to the questions.

Someone I miss very much:

_____

- How long have you known this person?
- When did you last see him or her?
- When will you see each other again?

Someone who gave me a special gift:

_____

- What was the gift?
- How long have you had it?
- What made the gift special?

Someone I'd like to know better:

_____

- How long have you known this person?
- When was the last time you spoke?
- What's he or she like?

Someone I've admired since I was a child:

_____

- When did you first meet this person?
- What do you admire about him or her?
- Do you share any of the same qualities?

B Pair work Interview your partner about each person. Ask questions for more information.

A: *Who is someone you miss very much?*
B: *I miss my grandmother very much.*
A: *How long have you known her?*
B: *I've known her since I was born! But I haven't seen her since April.*

A green quiz

A Pair work Interview your partner. Circle his or her answers.

HOW GREEN ARE YOU?
Try this quiz to find out.

1. You're leaving for the weekend, but you're not taking your computer. What do you do?
   a. Put it to "sleep."
   b. Shut it down.
   c. Turn it off and unplug it.

2. You're planning to go to a movie with several friends. What do you do?
   a. Go in separate cars.
   b. Meet and go in one car.
   c. Take public transportation.

3. You're walking and see some empty bottles on the sidewalk. What do you do?
   a. Leave the bottles there.
   b. Put them in a garbage can.
   c. Put them in a recycling bin.

4. Your office has a watercooler with plastic cups for people to use. What do you do?
   a. Use a different plastic cup each time.
   b. Use the same plastic cup all day.
   c. Use your own regular cup.

5. You're buying a magazine, and the cashier starts to put it in a bag. What do you do?
   a. Take the bag and throw it away later.
   b. Take the bag, but reuse it.
   c. Just take the magazine.

6. You have some old, unused medicine that you don't need. What do you do?
   a. Flush it down the toilet.
   b. Throw it in the garbage.
   c. Return it to a pharmacy.

7. You're making a salad and realize you don't have enough lettuce. What do you do?
   a. Get any lettuce at the nearest store.
   b. Buy organic lettuce at a farmer's market.
   c. Pick some lettuce from your own garden.

8. A company in your neighborhood is harming the environment. What do you do?
   a. Nothing.
   b. Tell your friends.
   c. Write a letter to the local newspaper about it.

B Pair work Score your partner's answers. How green is he or she? Are the results accurate?

a answers = 0 points
b answers = 1 point
c answers = 2 points

11–16 Congratulations! You lead a very green life.
6–10 You're green in some ways, but not in others.
0–5 You're not very green. It's not too late to change!

C Pair work What other things do you do to help the environment? Tell your partner.

Be an optimist!

A **Pair work** Add two situations to the chart. Then discuss what will, could, or might happen in each situation. Take notes.

If we . . . ,	we will . . .	we might . . .
eat too much fast food		
spend all day at the beach		
use cell phones in class		
read the news every day		
never study English		
watch too much TV		
don't get enough sleep		
spend too much time online		

A: *What do you think will happen if we eat too much fast food?*
B: *If we eat too much fast food, we'll gain weight.*

B **Group work** Share your ideas with another pair. Which ideas are the best? Do you have any other ideas?

What to do?

A **Group work** Imagine you have one of the relationship problems below. Your group gives you advice. Take turns.

My friend texts me constantly and then gets angry if I don't answer right away. Is it important to answer every text? I'm not sure what to do about this. I prefer to communicate by phone.

My sister has a new hairstyle, and I think it looks pretty awful. I don't really want to criticize her, but I think it's a good idea to say something to her. But what exactly do I say?

My co-worker won't talk to me. She says I gossiped about her. I guess I did, but it wasn't anything serious. It feels like she's judging me. I hope she can forgive me. After all, we need to work together.

My classmate always tries to copy my answers when we are taking tests or working on our own. It makes me angry. I don't want the teacher to think I'm cheating, too. Should I tell my teacher?

A: *My friend texts me constantly and then . . .*
B: *It's not important to answer every text. Just ignore them.*
C: *But it's not good to ignore them. Say something to your friend about it.*
D: *That's good advice. It's also a good idea to . . .*

B **Group work** Which advice was the best? Why? Tell your group.

"Maria gave the best advice. It's important to tell the truth."

C **Group work** Have you ever given relationship advice to someone? Who? What was the advice? Tell your group.

What do you think?

A Pair work Look at the picture. Make one speculation about each person. Use *must, could, can't, may,* or *might*.

A: *Diego is buying a dress, but it can't be for his wife. It's too small.*
B: *Right. He might be buying it for his daughter.*
A: *Yeah. And he must be rich. The store looks very expensive.*

B Group work Compare your speculations with another pair. Did you make any of the same ones?

Reflections

A Class activity Find classmates who answer "yes" to each question. Write their names and ask questions for more information.

Questions	Name	Extra information
1. Have you ever eaten an entire pizza by yourself?		
2. Do you learn better by studying in a group than by yourself?		
3. Did you teach yourself how to cook?		
4. Do you see yourself living in another country in five years?		
5. Have you ever traveled anywhere by yourself?		
6. Would you like to change something about yourself?		
7. Have you ever lived by yourself?		
8. Do you know someone who taught himself or herself a foreign language?		

A: *Have you ever eaten an entire pizza by yourself?*
B: *Yes, I have!*
A: *Wow! That's a lot of pizza. What kind of pizza was it?*
B: *It had cheese, pepperoni, onions, and peppers on it.*

B Share your information. What's the most interesting thing you learned? Who else in the class answered "yes" to each question?

Imagine that!

A Guess your partner's answers to the questions. Write your guesses in the chart.

Questions	My guesses	My partner's answers
1. What would you do if you saw your favorite celebrity?		
2. What would you do if your best friend moved to another country?		
3. How would you feel if someone brought up something embarrassing about you at a party?		
4. What would you do if you broke something expensive in a store?		
5. Where would you go if you had one week to travel anywhere in the world?		
6. What would you do if a friend borrowed some money from you and then didn't pay you back?		
7. What would you do if your grades in this class suddenly dropped?		

B **Pair work** Interview your partner. Complete the chart with his or her answers.
How many of your partner's answers did you guess correctly?

C **Class activity** Do any of your partner's answers surprise you? Would you and
your partner do any similar things? Tell the class.

Facts and opinions

A Group work Add two sets of questions about music to the list. Then discuss the questions. Ask follow-up questions to get more information.

1. What bands were formed in the 1960s? '70s? '80s? '90s? What was their music like?
2. What male singer do you think has a nice-sounding voice? What female singer?
3. What well-known singers or bands do you not like very much? Why not?
4. Were any record-breaking hits released last year? What did you think of the songs?
5. Was any truly awful music released in the past few years? What made it so terrible?
6. What was the last music awards show you saw on TV? Who was on it?
7. Who are the best-selling singers from your country? Do you enjoy their music?
8. What are some easily learned songs in your native language? Do you know all the words?
9. _____ ? _____ ?
10. _____ ? _____ ?

The Rolling Stones, 1960s

ABBA, 1970s

R.E.M., 1980s

The Spice Girls, 1990s

A: *The Rolling Stones were formed in the 1960s.*
B: *How was their music?*
A: *Their music was fantastic. It still is.*
C: *Can you name the band members?*

B Class activity Share any interesting information.

Find the differences

Student A

You and your partner have pictures of Monica and Victor, but they aren't exactly the same. Ask questions with *yet* to find the differences. Circle the items that are different.

see a movie

get a new stereo

download a song

send a text

buy a CD

sing a song

A: *Have Monica and Victor seen a movie yet?*
B: *No, they haven't. In my picture, they haven't seen it yet. They're going inside.*
A: *So that's different. In my picture, they're leaving the movie theater.*

Find the differences

Student B

You and your partner have pictures of Monica and Victor, but they aren't exactly the same. Ask questions with *yet* to find the differences. Circle the items that are different.

see a movie

get a new stereo

download a song

send a text

buy a CD

sing a song

A: *Have Monica and Victor seen a movie yet?*
B: *No, they haven't. In my picture, they haven't seen it yet. They're going inside.*
A: *So that's different. In my picture, they're leaving the movie theater.*

Travel partners

A Add three questions about travel preferences to the chart. Then check (✓) your answers.

When you travel, . . .	Me Yes	Me No	Name: _____ Yes	Name: _____ No
1. do you like being in a large group?	☐	☐	☐	☐
2. are you interested in meeting new people?	☐	☐	☐	☐
3. is saving money important to you?	☐	☐	☐	☐
4. do you like trying new foods?	☐	☐	☐	☐
5. is asking directions embarrassing to you?	☐	☐	☐	☐
6. do you like knowing your schedule in advance?	☐	☐	☐	☐
7. is camping more fun than staying in hotels?	☐	☐	☐	☐
8. do you enjoy shopping for souvenirs?	☐	☐	☐	☐
9. do you like big cities?	☐	☐	☐	☐
10. do you like going to clubs?	☐	☐	☐	☐
11. is seeing everything possible important to you?	☐	☐	☐	☐
12.	☐	☐	☐	☐
13.	☐	☐	☐	☐
14.	☐	☐	☐	☐

B Pair work Interview your partner. Complete the chart with his or her answers.

C Pair work Compare your answers. Would you make good travel partners? Why or why not?

A: *We wouldn't make good travel partners. You like being in a large group. I don't.*
B: *Yes, but we're both interested in meeting new people.*
A: *Well, that's true. And saving money is important to us.*

A backpacking trip

A **Pair work** Imagine someone is planning a two-week backpacking trip to your country. What rules and recommendations would you give for each category? Take notes.

Packing	Communication
Health and safety	**Places to stay**
Transportation	**Money**
Food	**Other**

B **Group work** Share your ideas with another pair. Did you have any of the same rules or recommendations? Can you think of any other rules or recommendations?

A: *You shouldn't pack too many clothes.*
B: *Yes, but you have to have enough clothes!*
C: *Also, you ought to bring your cell phone.*

Irregular verbs

Base form	Simple past	Past participle
be	was, were	been
become	became	become
break	broke	broken
build	built	built
buy	bought	bought
choose	chose	chosen
come	came	come
do	did	done
draw	drew	drawn
drink	drank	drunk
drive	drove	driven
eat	ate	eaten
fall	fell	fallen
feel	felt	felt
fly	flew	flown
forget	forgot	forgotten
get	got	gotten
give	gave	given
go	went	gone
hang	hung	hung
have	had	had
hear	heard	heard
hold	held	held
know	knew	known
leave	left	left

Base form	Simple past	Past participle
lose	lost	lost
make	made	made
meet	met	met
pay	paid	paid
put	put	put
read	read	read
ride	rode	ridden
run	ran	run
say	said	said
see	saw	seen
sell	sold	sold
send	sent	sent
sing	sang	sung
sit	sat	sat
sleep	slept	slept
speak	spoke	spoken
spend	spent	spent
stand	stood	stood
swim	swam	swum
take	took	taken
teach	taught	taught
think	thought	thought
wear	wore	worn
win	won	won
write	wrote	written

Adjective and adverb formations

Adjectives	Adverbs	Adjectives	Adverbs
agreeable	agreeably	immature	immaturely
amazing	amazingly	impatient	impatiently
ambitious	ambitiously	inconsiderate	inconsiderately
angry	angrily	indecisive	indecisively
brave	bravely	interesting	interestingly
careful	carefully	late	late
confident	confidently	lucky	luckily
considerate	considerately	mature	maturely
creative	creatively	nervous	nervously
curious	curiously	optimistic	optimistically
decisive	decisively	patient	patiently
disagreeable	disagreeably	quick	quickly
dishonest	dishonestly	rare	rarely
early	early	reliable	reliably
easy	easily	sad	sadly
enthusiastic	enthusiastically	serious	seriously
extreme	extremely	similar	similarly
fair	fairly	strange	strangely
fashionable	fashionably	stubborn	stubbornly
fast	fast	sudden	suddenly
fortunate	fortunately	surprising	surprisingly
glamorous	glamorously	unfair	unfairly
good	well	unfortunate	unfortunately
hard	hard	unreliable	unreliably
honest	honestly	wise	wisely

Answer key

Unit 7 Lesson D (page 71)

Listening

This personality test is just for fun. Don't take the answers *too* seriously!

1. This person is the most important person in your life.

2. If you see a big animal, you think you have big problems.

3. If you have a big house, you are very ambitious.

4. If the door is open, you're happy for people to visit anytime. If it's closed, you prefer people to call first.

5. If there is food or flowers on the table, you are very optimistic.

6. If the material is strong (like metal or plastic), you have a strong relationship with the person in number 1.

7. If you keep the cup, you want to keep a good relationship with the person in number 1.

Credits

Illustration credits

Tom Garrett: 13, 53, 63, 97; Kveta Jelinek: 91, 108 (top), 141; Kim Johnson: 2, 8, 18, 21, 28, 58, 68, 78, 88, 98, 108 (bottom), 118, 127, 128, 142, 143; Bill Ledger: 21, 29, 81, 101, 126; Dean Macadam: 8, 23, 31, 38, 48, 59, 87, 115, 125, 145; Garry Parsons: 7, 34, 95, 140, 147, 148; Maria Rabinky: 27, 100; Cristina Sampaio: 14, 54, 106, 136; Anastasia Vasilakis: 80

Photography credits

3 (clockwise from top left) ©Latin Stock Collection/Alamy; ©Alamy; ©Photo Edit; ©Huntstock/Getty Images; 4 (first row, left to right) ©Dorling Kindersley/Getty Images; ©Media Bakery; ©Media Bakery; (second row, left to right) ©Fuse/Getty Images; ©Media Bakery; ©Alamy; (third row, left to right) ©Geir Pettersen/Getty Images; ©Alamy; ©Media Bakery (fourth row, left to right) ©Alex Mares-Manton/Getty Images; ©Alamy; ©Getty Images; 6 (top) ©Frank Veronsky; (bottom row, left to right) ©Alamy; ©Fuse/Getty Images; ©Alamy; ©Fuse/Getty Images; ©Media Bakery; 9 ©Ivan Montero/Alamy; 11 ©Dean Mitchell/Alamy; 14 ©Michael Beiriger/Alamy; 16 (top) ©Frank Veronsky; (bottom row, left to right) ©Photodisc/Getty Images; ©Media Bakery; ©Erik Dreyer/Getty Images; 17 ©Getty Images; 18 (clockwise from top left) ©Alamy; ©Alamy; ©Media Bakery; ©Alamy; ©Tara Moore/Getty Images; ©Digital Vision/Getty Images; ©David J Spurdens/Getty Images; ©Food Pix/Getty Images; 19 ©Laurence Mouton/Getty Images; 24 (top row, left to right) ©Getty Images; ©Safia Fatimi/Getty Images; ©Trinette Reed/Getty Images; ©Comstock/Getty Images; ©Pando Hall/Getty Images; (middle row, left to right) ©Junichi Kusaka/Getty Images; ©Jupiter/Getty Images; ©Amana/Getty Images; ©Media Bakery; ©Alamy; (bottom row, left to right) ©Sir Lawrence Alma-Tadema/Getty Images; ©Elisabeth Vigée-Lebrun/The Royal Collection, London; ©Media Bakery; 25 ©Richard Simpson/Alamy; 26 (top, middle, people) ©Frank Veronsky; (top, middle, backgrounds) ©Alamy; (bottom row, all) ©Shutterstock; 27 (right to left) ©Istock; ©Media Bakery; ©Media Bakery; ©Shutterstock; ©Photo Edit; 30 (left to right) ©Istock; ©Alamy; 33 (clockwise from top left) ©Blaine Harrington III/Alamy; ©Joel Kiesel/Getty Images; ©Marissa Kaiser/Getty Images; ©Alamy; ©John Giustina/Getty Images; ©Jupiter; 34 ©Amana/Alamy; 36 (top to bottom) ©Frank Veronsky; ©Urban Zone/Alamy; 37 ©Digital Vision/Getty Images; 38 (clockwise from top left) ©Alamy; ©Media Bakery; ©Alamy; ©Media Bakery; ©Purestock/Alamy; ©Wolfram/Alamy; ©Steve Bly/Alamy; ©Paul Poplis/Getty Images; 39 ©Blend/Alamy; 40 (both) ©NASA; 41 ©Mike Brinson/Getty Images; 43 (clockwise from top left) ©Alamy; ©Lonely Planet; ©Massimo Pizzotti/Getty Images; ©Photo Library; ©Alamy; ©Newscom; 44 (top, clockwise from top left) ©Central America/Alamy; ©David Min/Getty Images; ©Alvey & Towers/Alamy; ©Media Bakery; ©Alamy; ©London Aerial Photo Library/Alamy; ©Andy Selinger/Alamy; (bottom) ©Photo Library; 46 (top to bottom) ©Alamy; ©Photo Library; 47 ©Michele Falzone/Alamy; 48 (top row, left to right) ©Image Broker/Alamy; ©Planet Observer/Getty Images; (middle row, left to right) ©John Lund/Getty Images; ©Alamy (bottom row, left to row) ©Alamy; ©Lonely Planet; ©Media Bakery; ©Jeremy Horner/Getty Images; 49 ©Corbis; 50 (left, top to bottom) ©Jupiter/Getty Images; ©Pal Teravagimov/Getty Images; ©Alamy; (right, top to bottom) ©Pascal Perret/Getty Images; ©Media Bakery; ©Media Bakery; ©Alamy; 51 (top to bottom) ©Stuart Westmorland/Getty Images; ©Alamy; 54 ©GoGo Images/Alamy; 56 (left to right) ©Glow Asia/Alamy; ©ML Harris/Getty Images; 58 (clockwise from top left) ©Photo Library; ©Bon Appetit/Alamy; ©Garry Wade/Getty Images; ©Alamy; ©Getty Images; ©Alamy; ©David Woolley/Getty Images; ©Media Bakery; 64 (left to right) ©Shutterstock; ©Alamy; 65 ©Radius Images/Alamy; 66 ©Frank Veronsky; 67 ©Alamy; 69 ©Media Bakery; 70 (all) ©Shutterstock; 71 (top to bottom) ©Alamy; ©Image Source/Alamy; 72 (both) ©Shutterstock; 73 (top row, both) ©Mark Jones/Ambius UK Ltd.; (middle row, left to right) ©DB/Alamy; ©Erik Von Weber/Getty Images; (bottom row, left to right) ©Richard Wong/Alamy; ©Della Huff/Alamy; 74 (top, clockwise from top left) ©Sven-Erik Arndt/Photo Library; ©Gallo Images – Neil Overy/Getty Images; ©Marc Hill/Alamy;

©Sam Toren/Alamy; ©Aerial Archives/Alamy; ©My Number/Alamy; ©Influx Productions/Getty Images; ©Peter Arnold/Alamy; ©Peter Erik Forsberg/Alamy; ©ICP/Alamy; (bottom, clockwise from top left) ©Influx/Getty Images; ©Doug Steley/Alamy; ©Alamy; ©Newscom; 76 Frank Veronsky; 77 ©Shutterstock; 78 (clockwise from top left) ©Travelwide/Alamy; ©Age Fotostock; ©Jeff Greenberg/Alamy; ©Alamy; ©Purestock/Getty Images; ©Alamy; ©Blend/Getty Images; ©Alamy; 81 (both) ©Action for Nature; 83 (clockwise from top left) ©Photo Library; ©Photodisc/Getty Images; ©Blend/Getty Images; ©Blend/Getty Images; 84 ©Alamy; 85 ©Alamy; 86 (top to bottom) ©Veer; ©Comstock/Getty Images; 87 (left to right) ©Jupiter/Getty Images; ©Veer; ©Media Bakery; ©Taxi Japan/Getty Images; 93 (clockwise from top left) ©Floresco Productions/Getty Images; ©Bernard van Dierendonck/Getty Images; ©Blend/Getty Images; ©Spencer Platt/Getty Images; ©Photo Edit; ©Photo Edit; 94 ©Stan Badz/Getty Images; 96 ©Frank Veronsky; 99 ©Alamy; 100 ©Courtesy of Mary King and Etsuko Shimabukuro; 103 (clockwise from top left) ©David Redfern/Getty Images; ©Retna; ©AP Wide World Photo; ©Bill Pugliano/Getty Images; ©Theo Wargo/Getty Images; ©John McCoy/Getty Images; ©M Becker/American Idol 2009/Getty Images; ©AP Wide World Photo; 104 (top to bottom) ©Janette Beckman/Getty Images; ©Dave Hogan/Getty Images; ©Newscom; ©Kevin Mazur/Getty Images; 105 ©AP Wide World Photo; 106 ©Digital Vision/Getty Images; 107 (iPad) ©Alamy; (all others) ©Shutterstock; 110 (top to bottom) ©Shutterstock; ©Media Bakery; ©Shutterstock; ©Alamy; ©Taxi Japan/Getty Images; ©Media Bakery; ©Alamy; ©Maria Teijeiro/Getty Images; 111 ©Alamy; 113 (all) ©Alamy; 114 (first row, left to right) ©JLImages/Alamy; ©Karina Tkach/Alamy; ©Keith Morris/Alamy; ©PCL/Alamy; (second row, left to right) ©Jim West/Alamy; ©Dave and Sigrun Tollerton/Alamy; ©Lou Linwei/Alamy; ©Travelscape Images/Alamy; (third row, left to right) ©Pontino/Alamy; ©Alamy; ©Photo Library; 116 ©Alamy; 117 (top to bottom) ©Photo Library; ©Alamy; 118 (clockwise from top left) ©Jupiter; ©Jupiter; ©Getty Images; ©Alamy; ©Alamy; ©LWA/Getty Images; ©Digital Vision/Getty Images; ©Sami Sarkis/Getty Images; 119 ©Alamy; 120 (clockwise from top left) ©Courtesy of Arlen Gargagliano; ©Media Bakery; ©Age Fotostock; ©Dreamstime; ©Age Fotostock; 121 (top to bottom) ©Age Fotostock; ©Alamy; 122 (all) Media Bakery; 123 (clockwise from top left) ©Media Bakery; ©Alamy; ©Stephen Simpson/Getty Images; 124 (left to right) ©Alamy; ©Media Bakery; ©Blend/Getty Images; 129 (left to right) ©Alamy; ©Alamy; ©Photodisc/Getty Images; 130 (clockwise from top left) ©Brett Froomer/Getty Images; ©AP Wide World Photo; ©Everett Collection; ©Shutterstock; ©Shutterstock; ©Shutterstock; 131 (left to right) ©Newscom; ©Age Fotostock; 132 (clockwise from top left) ©Shutterstock; ©Jupiter/Getty Images; ©Inmagine; ©Shutterstock; ©Alamy; ©Alamy; ©Shutterstock; ©Jupiter; 133 ©Alamy; 134 (clockwise from top left) ©Shutterstock; ©Jupiter/Getty Images; ©Inmagine; ©Shutterstock; ©Alamy; ©Alamy; ©Shutterstock; ©Jupiter; 135 (all) ©Alamy; 137 ©Science Photo Library/Getty Images; 138 (clockwise from top left) ©Alamy; ©Alamy; ©Purestock/Getty Images; ©Digital Vision/Getty Images; 139 (clockwise from top left) ©Inmagine; ©Shutterstock; ©Shutterstock; ©Media Bakery; ©Alamy; ©Alamy; ©Media Bakery; ©Inmagine; 144 (left to right) ©Peter Cade/Getty Images; ©Alamy; ©Media Bakery; 146 (clockwise from top left) ©Bentley Archive/Getty Images; ©Pictorial Press Ltd./Alamy; ©Trinity Mirror/Mirrorpix/Alamy; ©Stephanie Chernikowski/Getty Images; 149 (left to right) ©Alamy; ©Veer; ©Jeff Greenberg/Alamy; 150 (left to right) ©Alamy; ©Age Fotostock; ©Image Source/Getty Images

Four Corners

Jack C. Richards · David Bohlke

3B

Video Activity Sheets

CAMBRIDGE
UNIVERSITY PRESS

Signs of the Zodiac

Before you watch

A Label the pictures with the correct words. Then compare with a partner.

| a consultant | a graphic designer | a salesman | a student |

1. _____
2. _____
3. _____
4. _____

B Complete the sentences with the correct words. Then compare with a partner.

| adventurous | ambitious | creative | unreliable |

1. Often consultants are _____ people who work very hard to share their knowledge and advice with other people to help them succeed.

2. Graphic designers are usually _____ people. They use technology to make websites, magazines, and other things look very interesting and artistic.

3. Some people think that some salesmen can be _____ and that they don't always give you honest information about what you want to buy.

4. Students who study abroad in a different country are pretty _____. They're not afraid to go to new places, meet new people, and try new things.

While you watch

A Match the people and their zodiac signs.

Aries   Capricorn   Gemini   Virgo

1. Danielle's mother is a(n) _____.   a. Aries
2. Danielle's brother is a(n) _____.   b. Gemini
3. Danielle's father is a(n) _____.   c. Capricorn
4. Danielle is a(n) _____.   d. Virgo

B What are some characteristics of each sign? Write V (Virgos), A (Aries), C (Capricorns), or G (Geminis). (More than one answer is possible.)

1. _____ have difficulty sharing their feelings.

2. _____ are adventurous.

3. _____ are ambitious.

4. _____ are creative.

5. _____ are good at business.

6. _____ are sometimes unreliable.

7. _____ aren't open to new ideas.

8. _____ know what they want.

9. _____ want things done with no mistakes.

10. _____ worry too much.

C Check (✓) the correct answers.

	Danielle	Wendy	Max	Peter
1. Who has been a graphic designer for two years?	☐	☐	☐	☐
2. Who is taking a psychology class?	☐	☐	☐	☐
3. Who doesn't want to talk about Andy's promotion?	☐	☐	☐	☐
4. Who wants to put new wallpaper in the kitchen?	☐	☐	☐	☐
5. Who has owned a car dealership since 2003?	☐	☐	☐	☐
6. Who loves to try new things?	☐	☐	☐	☐
7. Who has to get back work?	☐	☐	☐	☐
8. Who has worked as a time management consultant for ten years?	☐	☐	☐	☐

After you watch

A Pair work Why does Danielle think her family members' personalities match the typical characteristics of their zodiac signs? Discuss and explain your ideas.

B Group work Discuss the questions.

- What do you know about zodiac signs?
- Do you know the characteristics of your zodiac sign? Do you think it matches your personality?
- Do you know anyone who matches the characteristics of his or her zodiac sign? How long have you known him or her?
- How do your family members and friends describe your personality? Do you agree with them?

Environmental superhero

Before you watch

A Match the words and the pictures. Then compare with a partner.

| a. candle | c. landfill | e. plant | g. recycling bins |
| b. ice | d. lightbulb | f. plastic bottles | h. superhero |

1. ☐

2. ☐

3. ☐

4. ☐

5. ☐

6. ☐

7. ☐

8. ☐

B Pair work Complete the sentences with the correct words from Part A. Then compare with a partner.

1. A _____ is a place where a town or group of people collects its garbage.

2. _____ is frozen water.

3. A _____ may go inside a lamp and provide light in a room.

4. Many people buy water and soda in _____.

5. The small fire on top of a _____ is called a flame; it gives off light.

6. A _____ is an imaginary person that saves and protects people or the earth.

7. A _____ could grow into an herb, a flower, or a vegetable.

8. In many public places, there are separate _____ for paper and plastic products.

While you watch

A What does Henry Green do to help the environment? Check (✓) the correct answers.

☐ He drives a hybrid car.

☐ He grows vegetables.

☐ He pays his bills online.

☐ He takes cloth bags to the supermarket.

☐ He uses an ice box to keep his food cold.

☐ He uses candles.

☐ He uses solar energy.

☐ He uses the recycling bins in his building.

B Circle the correct answers.

1. April is doing this video for _____
   a. her journalism class   b. her biology class   c. the school TV station

2. Henry Green is April's _____.
   a. grandfather   b. biology teacher   c. neighbor

3. April's nickname for Henry Green is _____.
   a. Environmental Man   b. Green Man   c. Environmental Impact Man

4. April says that compact fluorescent bulbs use _____ regular lightbulbs.
   a. less energy than   b. more energy than   c. the same energy as

5. April says that plastic bags and water bottles often end up in _____.
   a. landfills   b. schools   c. the ocean

6. April thinks Mr. Green is like a _____ to her.
   a. grandfather   b. friend   c. superhero

7. To thank Mr. Green, April gives him a _____.
   a. T-shirt   b. cloth shopping bag   c. candle

C Why does Mr. Green do these things? Match the things he does and the reasons.

1. He uses an ice box because _____.

2. He uses candles because _____.

3. He grows vegetables because _____.

4. He uses a cloth shopping bag because _____.

a. he doesn't want chemicals in his food.

b. he thinks people use too much plastic.

c. refrigerators use too much energy.

d. they use less energy than lightbulbs.

After you watch

Group work What's your opinion of what Mr. Green is doing? Discuss why you think each of his actions is a good idea or a bad idea.

- having an ice box instead of a refrigerator
- using candles instead of compact fluorescent bulbs
- growing vegetables at home
- taking a cloth shopping bag to the store

A: *I think using candles is a good idea. You can save energy if you use candles.*

B: *That's true. But candles could cause a fire if you aren't careful.*

She must be copying me!

Before you watch

A Match the words and the fashion items. Then compare with a partner.

a. bag

b. belt

c. bracelet

d. jacket

e. scarf

f. shirt

g. shoes

h. skirt

B People often *compliment* each other on fashion items, or say something nice to express that they like it. Are these compliments? Write Y (yes) or N (no).

1. "That jacket looks great on you!" _____

2. "Where did you buy that new bag?" _____

3. "I love your dress. It's really fashionable." _____

4. "Nice shirt! What a cool design!" _____

5. "I saw those same shoes in the store yesterday." _____

6. "That's a really pretty scarf. The color matches your eyes." _____

C **Pair work** Compliment your partner on two different fashion items.

While you watch

A What does Amanda have that's exactly like something Jessica or Beth has? Check (✓) the correct answers.

☐ bag	☐ a denim skirt	☐ a sweater
☐ bracelet	☐ a jacket	☐ a pair of red boots
☐ denim jeans	☐ a scarf	☐ a pair of red shoes

B Circle the correct answers.

1. Jessica's bag was a birthday present from _____.

   a. Amanda   b. her family   c. her mom

2. Beth thinks that Jessica's bag is beautiful and _____.

   a. retro   b. trendy   c. unusual

3. Beth _____ Amanda a few minutes ago.

   a. ran into   b. got together with   c. called

4. Mark is _____.

   a. Beth's friend   b. Amanda's boyfriend   c. Jessica's brother

5. Amanda thinks Jessica and Beth are _____ her.

   a. copying   b. lying to   c. helping

C Who thinks what? Check (✓) the correct answers.

	Jessica	Beth
1. Who thinks that Amanda must be copying her?	☐	☐
2. Who thinks that Amanda's behavior is a little strange these days?	☐	☐
3. Who thinks that they shouldn't judge Amanda too harshly?	☐	☐
4. Who thinks that Amanda broke up with Mark?	☐	☐
5. Who thinks that it's not good to criticize someone?	☐	☐
6. Who thinks that Amanda might be feeling upset or stressed out?	☐	☐
7. Who thinks that it's always good to forgive?	☐	☐

After you watch

Group work Discuss the questions. What do you think?

- Is Amanda copying Beth and Jessica?
- Are Beth and Jessica copying Amanda?
- Is it a coincidence? (No one is copying anyone; they all like the same things.)
- Has someone ever copied your clothes? How did you feel?
- Have you ever copied someone else's clothes, even a famous person's? What did you copy, exactly?
- What kinds of clothes (shirts, shoes, etc.) do you think people often copy? Why?

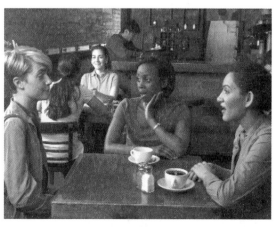

A cool accomplishment

Before you watch

A Complete the paragraph with the correct words. Then compare with a partner.

accomplished	busy	fashion designer
advice	college	studio

Martina has _____ something pretty cool! She graduated from Alicia's _____ seven years ago, and now she's a _____. Martina is working in her design _____. She is very _____ preparing for a fashion show, but she agreed to talk to Alicia. Alicia hopes Martina can give her some _____, because Alicia would like to become a fashion designer, too.

B Pair work Have you ever asked anyone for advice about how to be successful at school, your job, or your future career? What did they say you needed to do? Tell your partner.

While you watch

A Correct the false sentences.

1. Alicia is a high school student.

2. Martina had a lot of training when she started designing.

3. Martina's three words of advice to Alicia are: creativity, flexibility, and talent.

4. Alicia bought the dress she is wearing.

5. Martina thinks Alicia should plan a career in business.

B Circle the correct answers.

1. Martina says making her own clothes was a way to _____.

   a. make money   b. be creative   c. stay busy

2. Other students wanted to _____ the dresses and skirts Martina made.

   a. make   b. sell   c. buy

3. Martina describes the samples of fabric as chic, _____, and tacky.

   a. old-fashioned   b. trendy   c. retro

4. Martina had to do her first sketch over _____ times.

   a. three or four   b. five or six   c. ten or twelve

5. Martina says, "You have to be _____ and not afraid to say what you like."

   a. brave   b. patient   c. flexible

C Who makes each comment? Write A (Alicia) or M (Martina).

1. "I like the color." _____

2. "I could give this one some thought." _____

3. "That's terrible." _____

4. "We'll talk it over." _____

5. "I don't think we should do that." _____

6. "Your dress is lovely." _____

7. "I think you should give those shoes away." _____

8. "I'm not sure it's the best idea." _____

Alicia   Martina

After you watch

A Pair work How do you think Alicia felt after the interview with Martina? Why?
Do you think Alicia will become a fashion designer? Discuss your ideas.

B Write a job you have – or would like to have – in the circle. On the lines, write
three qualities that are necessary for success in that job.

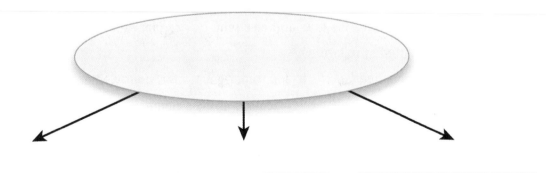

_____   _____   _____

C Pair work Compare and discuss your diagrams in Part B.

*"I would like to become a teacher after I graduate. To be a successful teacher, I think
you need creativity, enthusiasm, and dedication."*

I haven't made it yet.

Before you watch

A Complete the sentences with the correct words. Then compare with a partner.

| bass | costumes | drums | guitar | lyrics | pets |

1. A _____ is a type of _____. It has four strings and plays very low musical notes.

2. The _____ are the words to a song.

3. Dogs and cats are common _____ in the U.S.A.

4. _____ are clothes people wear in theatrical plays and other performances to look like someone else.

5. _____ are musical instruments that often provide the beat, or rhythm, to a song.

B Pair work Do you know anyone who is (or was) in a band? What is (or was) the band like? What kind of music do (or did) they play? Tell your partner.

a bass

drums

While you watch

A Circle the correct answers.

1. The Bulldogs are in the studio recording their _____ album.

   a. first   b. second   c. third

2. The band was named after their _____.

   a. pets   b. parents   c. favorite movie

3. The Bull Dogs describe their music as rock, hip-hop, _____.

   a. gospel, and jazz   b. hip-hop, and electronic   c. jazz, and pop

4. The band was started in college by _____.

   a. Chris, David, John, and Ian   b. four other guys   c. four women

5. They've sold _____ copies of their album.

   a. five   b. five hundred   c. five thousand

6. In college, they were given an award for _____.

   a. their record-breaking hit   b. best costume   c. worst-sounding band

7. Chris's song is about someone who _____.

   a. is in love   b. is a successful singer   c. wants to be a star

B Check (✓) the correct answers.

	Chris	David	Ian	John
1. Who hasn't finished his part on the last song yet?	☐	☐	☐	☐
2. Who has a cat named Bull?	☐	☐	☐	☐
3. Who says they're *not* a well-known band?	☐	☐	☐	☐
4. Who says they have a lot of fun?	☐	☐	☐	☐
5. Who is shopping?	☐	☐	☐	☐
6. Who has "a way with words" and writes the lyrics?	☐	☐	☐	☐

C Write T (true) or F (false).

1. John plays the drums. _____

2. Danielle doesn't really think "Dog" is a creative name for Chris's pet. _____

3. The band used to be called the Princesses. _____

4. The Bulldogs have sold many albums. _____

5. Chris finally sang his part of the song well, and the band recorded it. _____

After you watch

Group work Discuss the questions.

- What qualities does a band need to become successful?
- How would you describe the members of the Bulldogs?
- Do you think they have the qualities to become successful? Why or why not?
- Who is your favorite band? Why? Are they successful?

"I think you need talent to be a successful band. . . ."

Travels with Nick and Ben: Fish and chips

Before you watch

A Label the pictures with the correct words. Then compare with a partner.

| fish and chips | ketchup | high tea | lamb kebabs | vegetable curry | vinegar |

1. _____ 2. _____ 3. _____

4. _____ 5. _____ 6. _____

B Pair work Have you ever had the food items in Part A? If so, did you like them? If not, would you like to try them? Why or why not? Tell your partner.

While you watch

A Check (✓) the correct answers. (More than one answer is possible.)

	Ben	Nick
1. Who likes trying local foods on vacation?	☐	☐
2. Who likes to eat French fries with ketchup?	☐	☐
3. Who had Indian food at a restaurant on Brick Lane?	☐	☐
4. Who was only interested in eating fish and chips?	☐	☐
5. Who got a stomachache?	☐	☐
6. Who had high tea?	☐	☐
7. Who made fish and chips in the microwave?	☐	☐

B Write T (true) or F (false). Correct the false sentences.

1. When Nick goes on vacation, he loves visiting landmarks. _____

2. Nick and Ben prefer trying local foods when they travel. _____

3. French fries are called mashed potatoes in England. _____

4. People in England eat chips with ketchup. _____

5. Many people in London think of kebabs as British food. _____

C Circle the correct answers.

1. Nick says he does not like _____ on vacation.

    a. buying handicrafts   b. trying local food   c. traveling alone

2. Ben does *not* say the trip to London was _____.

    a. awesome   b. boring   c. delicious

3. Nick's lamb kebabs did *not* have any _____.

    a. fruit   b. lettuce   c. spicy sauce

4. Ben did *not* like the fish and chips from the _____.

    a. restaurant on Brick Lane   b. restaurant near Victoria Station   c. fast-food place

5. Ben and Nick do *not* say anything about _____ in the video.

    a. Buckingham Palace   b. Brick Lane   c. Hyde Park

After you watch

A Pair work If you went to London, would you have a trip like Nick and Ben's? How would your trip be the same? How would be it be different? Tell your partner.

B Write a city you know or have visited in the circle. On the lines, write two foods that are very good in that city and a good place to eat each one.

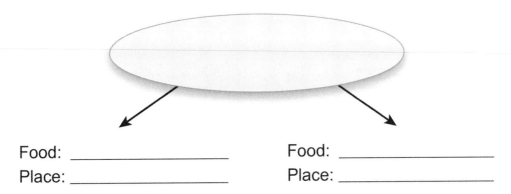

Food: _____   Food: _____

Place: _____   Place: _____

C Pair work Compare and discuss your diagrams in Exercise B.

"You have to try the barbecue chicken in Ubon, Thailand. You can eat it at the night market."

Credits

Photography credits

T-191 *(bottom)*, T-192, T-194, T-196, T-197, T-198, T-200, T-201 *(bottom)*
Video screen grabs courtesy of Steadman Productions, Boston, MA

Four Corners

Jack C. Richards · David Bohlke
with Kathryn O'Dell

3B

Workbook

Contents

Personalities

A You're extremely curious.

1 Put the letters in the correct order to make words for personality traits.

1. i a t s m i u b o   _____*ambitious*_____
2. b n s u b r t o   _____
3. e a c f l r u   _____
4. i o c m i t t i s p   _____

5. r s c i u u o   _____
6. o t i g u g o n   _____
7. u d s r t o n u a e v   _____
8. a i e o y n g s g   _____

2 Complete the sentences with the words for personality traits.

John sets high goals for himself. He's very

_____*ambitious*_____ . He's also extremely
         1

_____ . He loves learning
         2
about new things.

Celia is _____ , but she's also
         3

pretty _____ . She likes trying
         4
exciting sports, but she does them with attention
to detail.

Gina doesn't have a job right now, but she seems

OK. She always looks on the bright side, so she's

_____ about her future. She
        5
hardly ever worries. She's a very relaxed and

_____ person.
        6

Daniel can be very _____ .
         7
He never changes his mind about things! But

he's also very _____ .
        8
He's extremely friendly, so people like to be

around him.

3 Circle the correct words to complete the conversation.

Jane: How do your children like college, Rob?

Rob: Very much, thanks. Don is **carefully** /(**extremely**)
1
ambitious. He sets high goals for himself. You
know, he wants to be a pilot.

Jane: Wow. That's great. And the others?

Rob: Well, Greg **fairly** / **really** likes college. He's
2
early / **very** outgoing. He works **early** / **well** in
3   4
groups, but he thinks it's difficult to work alone, and you have do that a lot in college.

Jane: Well, it's good that he likes school.

Rob: And Ken is **pretty** / **slowly** curious. He likes to learn new things, so he loves school.
5
He's interested in many subjects, so he hasn't decided what career he wants yet.

Jane: That sounds like my son. And how's Brandon doing?

Rob: He's doing OK. He doesn't work **very** / **well** without direction, but if you tell him
6
what to do, he does it **really** / **well**. Ken and Brandon go to the same college,
7
so they help each other.

Jane: That's nice.

4 Rewrite the sentences to correct the mistakes in the order of the words.
Sometimes there is more than one mistake in the sentence.

1. Steven and Susan are curious extremely about the new student in class.

   Steven and Susan are extremely curious about the new student in class.

2. Mario doesn't play well the guitar when he's nervous.

   _____

3. Tae-ho's parents are important very to him.

   _____

4. Kendra is outgoing fairly, and she makes easily new friends.

   _____

5. Pam quickly drives, but she's careful pretty.

   _____

6. Jacob slowly is moving, so he'll be late for his doctor's appointment this morning.

   _____

5 Look at the chart. Write sentences about Shan.

	easily	very	fairly	hard
1. make friends	✓			
2. ambitious			✓	
3. study during the week				✓
4. not stubborn		✓		
5. not work on the weekends				✓
6. outgoing		✓		
7. optimistic			✓	
8. not share her feelings	✓			

1. *Shan makes friends easily.* _____

2. *She is* _____

3. _____

4. _____

5. _____

6. _____

7. _____

8. _____

6 Complete the sentences so they are true for you. Use some of the adverbs from the box.

Example: *I'm pretty ambitious.* or *I'm not very ambitious.*

carefully	(not) extremely	pretty	slowly
completely	fairly	quickly	(not) very
easily	hard	(not) really	well

1. I'm _____ ambitious.

2. I'm _____ serious about learning English.

3. I'm _____ optimistic about my future.

4. I make new friends _____ .

5. I'm _____ curious about math and science.

6. I work _____ when I do my homework.

B In my opinion, . . .

1 Complete the conversations with phrases from the box. Use each expression once.
More than one answer is possible.

Don't you agree	Don't you think that's true	In my opinion,
Don't you think so	If you ask me,	Maybe it's just me, but I think

Olivia: Heather, what do you think of this statue?

Heather: Oh, it's very interesting. _Don't you agree_ ?

1

Olivia: No, not really. _____ it's ugly.

2

Olivia: And look at this painting. What do you think of it?

Heather: I like it, but it's a little weird. _____ ?

3

Olivia: _____ it's pretty amazing!

4

Olivia: Wow. Look at this. It's great! _____ ?

5

Heather: No, I don't. _____ it's disgusting!

6

2 What do you think? Complete the conversation with your own idea. Use an expression
for giving an opinion.

Olivia: Hey, what do you think of this painting?

Heather: Oh, it's nice. Don't you agree?

You: _____

_____

_____

C We've been friends for six years.

1 Look at the dictionary definitions for personality traits. Write the correct words.

1. a *greeable* _____ (adj) friendly and pleasing

2. c_____ (adj) thinking of the needs of others

3. d_____ (adj) making decisions quickly

4. f_____ (adj) treating people equally or right

5. h_____ (adj) truthful

6. m_____ (adj) behaving in a responsible way

7. p_____ (adj) waiting without getting annoyed

8. r_____ (adj) doing what is expected or promised

2 Complete the sentences with the correct words for personality traits. Use the opposites of the words from Exercise 1.

1. John is sometimes _____ *dishonest* _____ . He doesn't always tell the truth.

2. Some people in the group were _____ , so we didn't become friends.

3. Jack is pretty _____ . He didn't come to pick me up at the airport. I had to take a taxi home.

4. Amanda is 17, but she's pretty _____ . She acts like she's only 12 or 13.

5. Please don't be _____ ! You don't have to wait much longer. I'm almost finished.

6. Bob and I are often _____ . We hardly ever make decisions quickly!

7. Peter is a very _____ and _____ person. He never thinks about other people's needs, and he doesn't treat people equally.

3 Complete the chart. Write the words from the box in the correct column.

✓ 2010	a few days	last night	two months
4:30	five hours	a long time	Wednesday
December	I was 18	quite a while	a year

I've lived here for . . .	I've known him since . . .
	2010

4 Look at the calendar and the information about Vanessa. Today is Saturday. Complete the sentences with *since*. Then rewrite them with *for*.

Monday	Tuesday	Wednesday	Thursday	Friday
got a new job	met Greg at work	had a blind date with Carlos	stopped talking to Greg	got sick

1. Vanessa has had a new job *since Monday* .

    Vanessa has had a new job for five days.

2. She has known Greg _____ .

    _____

3. She has known Carlos _____ .

    _____

4. She's hasn't talked to Greg _____ .

    _____

5. She's been sick _____ .

    _____

5 Write sentences with the words in parentheses. Use the present perfect with *for* or *since*.

1. (Yolanda / be / friends with Jenna / a long time)

   Yolanda has been friends with Jenna for a long time.

2. (I / not see / Jun / three days)

   _____

3. (I / not have / an argument with my parents / I was a kid)

   _____

4. (Tom and Melissa / be / married / three years)

   _____

5. (Matt / not eat / sushi / he was in Japan)

   _____

6. (Sandra / know / Katia / 2005)

   _____

6 Read the email. Then answer the questions. Use *for* or *since*.

Dear Uncle Henry,

How are you? I'm great! As you know, I got married a week ago! I'm sorry you couldn't come to the wedding. Can you believe that I met Julie at your son's wedding in 2001?

Julie and I are on vacation now. We got to Hawaii four days ago. It's beautiful here! Unfortunately, Julie got sick on Wednesday, so we're in the doctor's office now. We got here at 1:00 p.m., and we have to wait a little longer to see the doctor. The office is pretty busy. Julie's mother called five minutes ago, and they're talking on the phone now. Julie's going to be OK. She probably had some bad seafood.

I have to go. They say I have to turn off my computer!

Take care,

Josh

1. How long has Josh been married?   *He's been married for a week.*

2. How long has Josh known Julie?   _____

3. How long have Josh and Julie been in Hawaii?   _____

4. How long has Julie been sick?   _____

5. How long have they been in the doctor's office?   _____

6. How long has Julie been on the phone?   _____

D · *What is your personality?*

1 Read the article. Then answer the questions.

1. Which color in the article do you like best? _____

2. Are you like (or not like) the personality description for that color? _____

What does your favorite color say about your personality?

We all have a favorite color. But did you know that your favorite color might say something about your personality?

WHITE. White is a peaceful color. You like simple things. You are extremely fair, and you always tell the truth. You also want your friends to be truthful.

RED. Red is a strong color. You are outgoing and like meeting new people. You are optimistic and very ambitious. You are also decisive, and you are sometimes stubborn.

ORANGE. You are pretty easygoing and you like to be agreeable. You are curious about people and like to learn about them. You have a lot of friends. You want people to notice you, and you sometimes dress in flashy clothes!

YELLOW. Yellow is a happy color. You are very funny and have a lot of friends. You are pretty adventurous, too! But

sometimes you are not very responsible. That's not always a bad thing because taking risks is fun if you are careful.

GREEN. Green is the color of nature. You're fairly curious about the world. You like to be outdoors, and you are also adventurous. You are patient, kind, and easygoing.

BLUE. Blue is also a color in nature. Like "green" people, you are also very patient. You are reliable, and you want your friends to be considerate. You probably aren't very adventurous.

PURPLE. Purple is a color for creative people. You like music and the arts. You enjoy visiting museums and taking pictures.

BLACK. Black is a mysterious color. You have secrets. You are very curious about many different things.

2 Read the article again. Then circle the correct word to complete each sentence.

1. People who like white are **honest** / dishonest.

2. People who like yellow **like** / **don't like** trying new things.

3. People who like red are **good** / **bad** at making decisions.

4. People who like blue probably **like** / **don't like** trying new things.

5. People who like purple are usually **creative** / **boring**.

6. People who like black often **have** / **don't have** secrets.

The environment

A *Going green*

1 Complete the text with one word from box A and one word from box B.

A	e-	global	hybrid	~~nuclear~~	organic	plastic	recycling	solar	wind
B	bags	bin	car	~~energy~~	energy	farm	food		warming	waste

Easy Ways You Can Help the Environment

1. Many people don't like *nuclear energy* .
   They prefer to get their electricity from a
   _____ .

2. Buy and drive a _____ . They
   don't use as much gas as other cars, and they
   cause less pollution.

3. Take your own cloth bags to the supermarket.
   Don't use _____ .

4. Cook and eat _____ . It is safer
   for the environment.

5. Regular lightbulbs are not good for the
   environment. Use CFLs instead. This will help
   reduce _____ .

6. Put a large _____ in your house,
   and recycle paper, glass, and plastic.

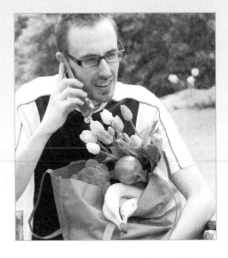

7. When you buy a new computer, don't throw the
   old one away. If it still works, give it to a friend.
   This will help reduce _____ .

8. Use _____ to dry your clothes.
   Put your towels, blouses, shirts, pants, and even
   jeans on a clothesline to dry in the sun.

2 Write C (count noun) or N (noncount noun).

1. energy   _N_   4. recycling bin _____   7. bottle _____

2. e-waste _____   5. pollution _____   8. landfill _____

3. lightbulb _____   6. plastic bag _____   9. plastic _____

3 Complete the sentences with *fewer* or *less*.

1. The world would be a better place with _____*less*_____ e-waste.

2. People should use _____ plastic bags.

3. There should be _____ pollution in big cities.

4. There are _____ wind farms in the United States than in Europe.

5. Many people are trying to use _____ energy in their homes.

6. I'm sure you'll use _____ gas with your hybrid car.

4 Complete the letter with *too many* or *too much*.

LETTER TO THE EDITOR

June 17

I read the article *Building Goes Up Green* yesterday. It was very interesting, and I'm glad we're going to have a shopping mall that is better for the environment. There are _____*too many*_____ buildings in this city that are bad for the environment. Most
                       1
buildings use _____ energy, so it's important that the new
                        2
buildings will use solar energy.

I think that the mall has a lot of creative ideas to help the environment in other ways, too. Using cloth bags is a wonderful idea. People will save money and help the environment at the same time. There are _____ plastic bags in
                                                              3
landfills around the world, and every little bit helps! I also think there are

_____ landfills in this city, so I'm glad the shopping mall plans to
            4
have a recycling center, too. People throw away _____ garbage,
                                                              5
and I hope this will help more people recycle.

I hope you write more articles about the mall.

Sincerely,

Dennis Armstrong

Environmental Student

5 Look at the web post. Then write sentences about what Mi-yon has. Use *not enough* or *too many*.

> Thank you, friends! I almost have enough recycled things for my art project, but I still need a few more. If you have any of them, please send them to me at 556 Claremont Street.
>
> | | I needed | Now I have | I still need |
> |---|---|---|---|
> | 1. plastic bottles | 100 | 85 | 15 |
> | 2. glass bottles | 25 | 30 | 0 |
> | 3. plastic bags | 250 | 199 | 51 |
> | 4. old lightbulbs | 50 | 40 | 10 |
> | 5. old toothbrushes | 30 | 42 | 0 |
> | 6. old CDs | 175 | 170 | 5 |
>
> Thanks!
>
> Mi-yon Kam, Green Artist

1. _Mi-yon doesn't have enough plastic bottles._
2. _She has too_ _____ .
3. _____
4. _____
5. _____
6. _____

6 Answer the questions with your own information. Use quantifiers.

Example: _Yes, I do. I recycle paper. I could recycle more glass and plastic._ or
No, I don't, and I don't use enough cloth bags.

1. Do you recycle? _____
2. Do you have recycling bins in your home? _____
3. Does your town have enough recycling centers? _____
4. Do you use things in your home to save energy? _____
5. How much pollution is in your town? _____
6. How could you make less garbage in your home? _____

B I'd rather not say.

Complete each conversation with the expressions in the box.

| I'd say about   I'd rather not answer that |

A. Larry: Hi, Kim. How's your new house?

    Kim: It's great. We love the solar roof.

  Larry: How much is your electric bill now?

    Kim: _I'd_ _____ $40 a month.

                 1

  Larry: Wow! That's cheap. How much did the solar roof cost?

    Kim: _____ , but it was a

                 2

good purchase. We save money each month, and we help the environment!

| I'd say maybe   I'd rather not say |

B. Alice: Hi, Hala. Where are you going?

    Hala: I'm going to the mall.

  Alice: What are you going to buy?

    Hala: Actually, _____ . It's a surprise for

                     1

my sister's birthday.

  Alice: Oh, OK. Well, I'll see you at her party. What time should I get there?

    Hala: Oh, _____ around 6:00 p.m.

               2

  Alice: OK.

| probably   I'd prefer not to say |

C. Peng: Wow, Steve. I like your new car.

  Steve: Thanks!

    Peng: When did you get it?

  Steve: Um, _____ about a month ago.

               1

    Peng: Is it a hybrid car?

  Steve: No, it isn't. The hybrid cars were too expensive.

    Peng: Oh, that's too bad. How much do you spend on gas?

  Steve: _____ , but definitely too much!

              2

What will happen?

1 Circle the correct verb to complete each tip for helping the environment.

1. (Use)/ Grow / Take a clothesline.

2. Fix / Buy / Use leaky faucets.

3. Take / Pay / Buy local food.

4. Grow / Take / Pay public transportation.

5. Use / Pay / Fix rechargeable batteries.

6. Pay / Fix / Use cloth shopping bags.

7. Grow / Pay / Use your own food.

8. Take / Fix / Pay bills online.

2 Look at the pictures. Complete each sentence with the simple present of one tip from Exercise 1.

1. Debbie *uses a*

   clothesline   .

2. Martin _____

   _____ .

3. Many people in big cities

   _____ .

4. Wesley _____

   _____ .

5. Rita _____

   _____ .

6. Andy _____

   _____ .

3 Complete the story. Change the main clause of the last sentence to an *if* clause in the next sentence.

If I get a new car, I'll buy a hybrid car.

1. _If I buy a hybrid car_____, I'll save money on gas.

2. _If I save_____, I'll have more money to spend.

3. _____, I'll buy a new cell phone.

4. _____, I'll recycle my old cell phone.

5. _____, there will be less e-waste.

6. _____, the world will be a better place!

4 Write sentences with the phrases in the chart. Use the first conditional and *will*. Write each sentence two ways.

	Who	The condition	The result
1.	Robert	use rechargeable batteries	buy fewer batteries
2.	Emma	take public transportation	use less gas
3.	Tom and Jackie	have enough money	buy a hybrid car
4.	You	buy local food	get good fruit and vegetables
5.	We	recycle more bottles	help the environment

1. _If Robert uses rechargeable batteries, he'll buy fewer batteries._

    Robert will buy fewer batteries if he uses rechargeable batteries.

2. _____

    _____

3. _____

    _____

4. _____

    _____

5. _____

    _____

5 Write the answers to the questions. Use the first conditional and the words in parentheses.

www.ecoblog.cup/Q&A

We want your opinions! Please tell us what you think!

What do you think will happen if more people recycle?

Marc67: _If more people recycle, we might have less garbage_ .
(have less garbage / we / might)

SSGreen: _If more people_ .
(could / help the environment / it)

What do you think will happen if our town starts a wind farm?

EcoJoe: _____ .
(use less energy / we / may)

EvaR22: _____ .
(be more jobs / might / there)

What do you think will happen if the big supermarket closes?

SSGreen: _____ .
(we / may / buy more local food)

EvaR22: _____ .
(some people / get upset / might)

6 Answer the questions with your own opinion. Use *will, may, might,* or *could*. Use each word at least once.

Example: _If people stop driving cars, there will be less pollution._ or

Many people might lose their jobs if people stop driving cars.

1. What will happen if people stop driving cars? _____

2. What will happen if everyone buys a bike? _____

3. What will happen if we don't have clean water? _____

4. What will happen if people don't fix leaky faucets? _____

5. What will happen if there is no more pollution? _____

6. What will happen if people have to pay for plastic bags in stores? _____

7. What will happen if you grow your own food? _____

8. What will happen if people buy new computers every year? _____

D Finding solutions

1 Read the article. Then check (✓) the chapters that might be in Chelsea Thomson's book.

1. ☐ How to Use Less Energy
2. ☐ How to Waste Time
3. ☐ How to Recycle More
4. ☐ Buy More Than You Need

5. ☐ How to Have More Garbage
6. ☐ How to Use Your Car Less Often
7. ☐ Where to Buy Local Food
8. ☐ Kinds of Food You Can Grow at Home

Dear Readers,

My new book, *Going Completely Green*, is finished! As the title says, I decided to go completely green for a month – no electricity, no running water, no car, no phone, no computer! I didn't even use anything with batteries. It was very difficult, and I decided to write a book about my experience. During the day, I wrote on paper with a pencil. When I wanted to sharpen my pencil, I remembered my pencil sharpener uses electricity. I had to sharpen it with a knife! At night, I used a candle for light. I washed all of my clothes by hand with water from the river behind my house, and then I put them on a clothesline. I walked to a local farm to buy food. I ate mostly fruits and vegetables. I only ate meat about five times, and I cooked it over a fire in my yard. The hardest part was not talking to friends and family on the phone or emailing them. My best friend lives an hour away by car, so I didn't communicate with her at all.

In my opinion, it is impossible to live completely green for a long time, but there are many things you can do. Now, I try to work with the lights off for most of the day. I'm driving my car again, but I try to walk or ride my bike when I only have to go a short distance. I buy more local food now, too. I have to use my computer for work, but I use it for fewer hours each day. I also turn it off when I'm not home. There are many things you can do to use less energy and water. This book will help you learn how to live a greener life. If you follow the steps in my book, you'll really help the environment. Oh, and if you buy my book, you might want to read it by candlelight to save energy!

Chelsea Thomson

2 Read the article again. Rewrite the sentences to correct the underlined mistakes.

1. Chelsea went green for <u>two months</u>.   *Chelsea went green for a month.*

2. She wrote <u>on a computer</u>. _____

3. She washed her clothes <u>on a clothesline</u>. _____

4. She thinks it's impossible <u>to work with the lights off</u>. _____

5. Now she <u>drives her car</u> for short distances. _____

6. She turns her computer off if <u>she's working</u>. _____

Relationships

A Healthy relationships

1 Complete the sentences and the puzzle with the correct words. Use words about relationship behaviors.

Across

3. Mr. Jenkins said I didn't do a good job. He always finds things in my work to _____ .

6. Don and Greg _____ all the time. They never listen to each other.

7. Gina is really sorry. She's going to _____ to Kate.

8. Kate knows Gina is sorry. She's going to _____ her.

Down

1. My mother likes to _____ my friends. She always tells me if they are good or bad friends.

2. Please don't _____ . I know you're not being honest.

3. Josh and Dan usually _____ by email, but they sometimes talk on the phone.

4. I want to go to a restaurant, and you want to go to the park. Let's _____ and eat food in the park!

5. Shannon talks about everyone! I hate when people _____ .

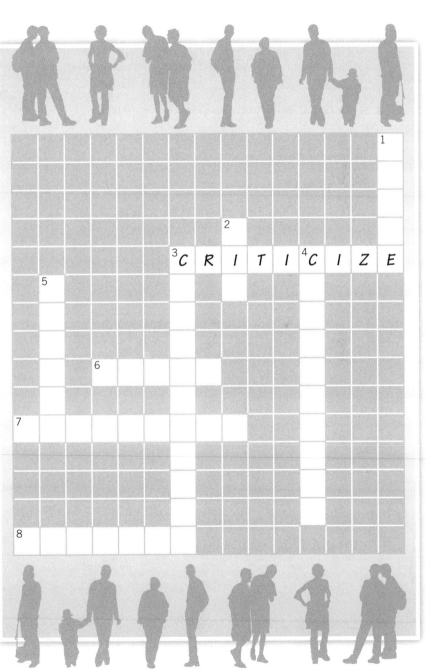

2 Complete the advice column. Use the infinitive forms of the correct verbs from the box.

| apologize | argue | be | communicate | compromise | ✓lie |

Ask Lee

Dear Lee,

Sometimes it's difficult to tell my parents the truth. I'm a pretty good son, but I make mistakes. I don't want my parents to get upset. I know that it's not good __to lie__₁, but sometimes it's hard to be honest. What's your advice?

        – Stressed-Out Son

Dear Stressed-Out Son,

It's not always easy _____₂ honest, but you should try. It's very important _____₃ with your parents. If you say you made a mistake, it might help them understand. They used to be young, and they made mistakes, too.

Dear Lee,

My friends and I are planning a vacation, and we're arguing. Two people want to go to the beach, and one person wants to go hiking. What should we do?

        – Ralph

Dear Ralph,

It's never a good idea _____₄ with your friends. It's important _____₅ . Why don't you go to a park with mountains near the ocean, like the Manuel Antonio National Park in Costa Rica? You can hike in the mountains and go to the beach!

Dear Lee,

I gossiped about my friend to some other people. I feel terrible, and now she won't talk to me. Please help!

        – Pamela G.

Dear Pamela,

When someone is upset with you, it's useful _____₆ . If she doesn't want to talk to you, tell her you're sorry in an email. If she knows how you feel, she may forgive you.

3 Put the words in the correct order to make a sentence.

1. It's / to help / your neighbors / a good idea / .

    It's a good idea to help your neighbors.

2. to apologize / It's / nice / when you're wrong / .

    _____

3. with your teacher / not good / It's / to argue / .

    _____

4. It's / to compromise / important / with your friends / .

    _____

5. helpful / It's / in class / to listen carefully / .

    _____

6. never a good idea / about your friends / It's / to gossip / .

    _____

4 Complete the sentences with your own ideas. Use expressions from the box.

| It's (not) a good idea | It's (not) helpful | It's (not) useful |
| It's (not) good | It's (not) important | |

Example: **At school:** _It's important to be on time._

At school:

1. _____ (be) on time.

2. _____ (use) a dictionary in class.

With your friends:

3. _____ (communicate) dishonestly
   or impatiently.

4. _____ (plan) activities that
   everyone enjoys.

At a library:

5. _____ (talk) quietly.

6. _____ (write) in the books.

B I'm really sorry.

1 Circle the correct phrase to complete each conversation.

A.

Kelly: Hi, Doug. **That's OK** /(**I'm really sorry**)
I missed your birthday.
1

Doug: **There's no need to apologize.** / **I'm sorry.**
2

Kelly: Well, it's not nice to miss a friend's birthday.

Doug: Please, Kelly. **I'm sorry.** / **Don't worry about it.**
3

Kelly: OK. But let's celebrate on Friday.

Doug: Great!

B. **Kelly:** Hi, Doug. **There's no need to**
apologize / **I'm sorry**, but I can't
1
make it on Friday.

Doug: **That's OK.** / **My apologies.**
2

Kelly: No, it's not. I feel terrible.
My apologies. / **Don't worry about**
3
it. Can you come over on Saturday?
I'll make dinner!

Doug: OK. That sounds great.

2 Complete the conversations. Use some of the expressions from Exercise **1**
and your own ideas.

A.   **You:** I missed your party. _____ .
1

Friend: Oh, _____ . What happened?
2

You: _____ .
3

Friend: That's too bad.

B. **Friend:** I am very late. _____ .
1

You: _____ . Is everything all right?
2

Friend: Not really. _____ .
3

You: Oh. Too bad!

C *That can't be the problem.*

1 Complete each question with the correct word from the box.

✓after	into	together
along	on	up
by	on	up

1. Do you take _____*after*_____ anyone in your family? Who?

2. Have you ever been picked _____ in school? By whom?

3. Do you get _____ well with your friends?

4. Have you ever broken _____ with a boyfriend or girlfriend? Who?

5. How often do you get _____ with friends each month? What do you do?

6. Do you like it when friends drop _____ and don't call first? Who does this?

7. Who is the last person you ran _____ when you were shopping?

8. Do you know anyone who is immature and needs to grow _____ ? Who?

9. Who is the person you count _____ the most?

2 Answer the questions in Exercise 1 with your own information. Use phrasal verbs, and add more information when possible.

Example: *Yes, I do. I take after my mother. We're friendly and outgoing. I look*
          like her, too.   or
          No, I don't. But I'd like to take after my father. He's really intelligent.

1. _____

2. _____

3. _____

4. _____

5. _____

6. _____

7. _____

8. _____

9. _____

3 Complete the sentences with the correct words from the box.

| can't   may   ✓must |

1. Cindy _____**must**_____ get along well with her family. She's at her parents' house every weekend.

2. I'm not sure, but I think I _____ know where the restaurant is.

3. Mark _____ be breaking up with me! He loves me!

| could   might not   must not |

4. Bev _____ come to work today. She felt sick yesterday.

5. Josh _____ be coming to the party. It started an hour ago, and he's not here.

6. You _____ run into Dan at the mall. I think he's shopping today.

4 Complete the conversation with *must*, *can't*, or *might*.

Sandra: Good morning, Paul. Do you know where Dan is? I didn't see his car outside.

Paul: I'm not sure. He _____**might**_____ be at a
$$_1$$
doctor's appointment.

Sandra: No, he _____ have a doctor's
$$_2$$
appointment today. I have all his appointments in my calendar.

Paul: You're right. He _____ be taking
$$_3$$
the bus today. The buses are often late.

Sandra: Well, he _____ have a good reason. He's never late.
$$_4$$

Paul: Wait! My phone's ringing. It _____ be Dan. Let me see. . . .
$$_5$$
No. It _____ be Dan. It's not his number.
$$_6$$

Sandra: Well, you should answer it! Dan _____ be calling from a different
$$_7$$
phone if there's a problem.

A minute later . . .

Paul: Yes. It was Dan. He _____ be feeling pretty stressed. He ran out
$$_8$$
of gas and had to ask a stranger to drive him to a gas station. But he left his cell phone in his car, so he had to ask the stranger to use her phone.

5 Answer the questions with your own ideas. Use words from the box to speculate and to say how sure you are.

can't	could	may (not)	might (not)	must (not)

Example: *I don't know. She might be looking for some money.* or

I see her car. She must be looking for her keys.

1. What is the woman looking for?

_____

2. What animal is it?

_____

3. Why is the boy crying?

_____

4. Why are they arguing?

_____

5. Why is the woman late?

_____

6. Where are they going?

_____

D Getting advice

1 Read the advice. Who is the speaker giving the advice to? Write the correct heading from the magazine article.

1. "I'm sorry, but you need to get more organized. Your work is often late." _To a co-worker_

2. "It must feel bad that James doesn't want to play with you. Could you ask Kahil?" _____

3. "I don't think he's good for you. Do you ever think about breaking up?" _____

How to Give Advice

Everyone has an opinion, but sometimes it's not easy to give advice. This is really true for important relationships. Here are some tips on how you can give advice in different relationships.

To a child If you aren't careful, children might get angry when you give them advice. They are often immature, and they don't understand that you want to help. It's useful to tell them you understand what they are going through before you give them advice. Be considerate, think about how they might feel, and remember that their opinions matter. It's not helpful to speak loudly or to criticize; this makes children feel worse, and they might not listen to you.

To a co-worker It can be difficult to give advice to people at work, so it's often good to apologize first. For example, say, "I'm sorry, but I think you could . . ." And remember that it's never a good idea to judge people. Give advice about what you think should change about the person's work, not about the person! Also remember that in work situations, you often have to compromise. You may give advice, but the person might not take it!

To a friend Friends can be the hardest people to give advice to. It's important to be honest, but you should also be kind. When you give advice to a friend, don't argue. Try to communicate with your friend. Ask questions and really understand your friend's problem before you give advice.

These tips are useful in other types of relationships, too. The important thing to remember is to be patient with others, and give them a chance to respond to your advice. It's also helpful to give advice when the person is ready to listen. Don't give advice when the person is extremely upset or stressed. Try to find a time when he or she is more relaxed.

2 Read the article again. Check (✓) what the writer says about giving advice.

1. Don't argue. ☑
2. You may need to compromise. ☐
3. You might need to get angry. ☐
4. Be honest. ☐
5. Don't give advice about work. ☐
6. Ask questions. ☐

Living your life

A *He taught himself.*

1 Complete the puzzle with words for qualities for success. What's the mystery word?

1. a strong interest in something
2. the quality of showing no fear
3. the ability to change easily
4. a commitment to something
5. the belief that you can succeed
6. the ability to develop original ideas

```
¹E  N  T  H  U  S  I  A  S  M
 ²
³
      ⁴
   ⁵
 ⁶
```

2 Circle the correct words to complete the article.

Man Saves Friend

Farmers Jim Rolland and Ryan Jensen were trying to take soybeans out of a large bin, but they wouldn't come out. Jim Rolland was **(confident)** / **confidence** that he could fix the problem, but his **confident** / **confidence** got him in trouble.
1   2
He climbed some stairs and went into the bin. The beans moved and covered him completely!

Ryan Jensen told another worker to call for help. Then he had a **creative** / **creativity** idea. He wasn't
3
sure it was **wise** / **wisdom**, but he also went into the bin. He got on his stomach on top of the
4
beans. For four hours, he moved beans so Rolland could breathe. His **dedicated** / **dedication** and
5
brave / **bravery** saved his friend's life.
6

Rescue workers finally came. They removed the beans and helped Rolland out of the bin. He was fine, and he was happy to have **talented** / **talent** people help him.
7

3 Put the words in the correct order to make sentences.

1. a picture of / art class / myself / I / painted / in / .

   I painted a picture of myself in art class.

2. by / The / isn't / itself / computer / going to work / .

   _____

3. brave / herself / doesn't / mother / My / consider / .

   _____

4. Japanese / themselves / taught / Kyle / and Mick / .

   _____

5. blame / Don't / for / my / yourselves / problems / !

   _____

6. did / Chris / When / hurt / himself / ?

   _____

7. yourself / by / draw / Did / you / that picture / ?

   _____

8. enjoyed / We / on / ourselves / trip to New York / our / .

   _____

4 Complete the sentences with the correct reflexive pronouns.

> What do people like to do by _____ _themselves_ _____ ? Here's what some
> of our readers said:
>
> - I like to travel by _____ . I always meet interesting people,
>   and sometimes they teach me words of wisdom. (Tom P., Chicago)
>
> - My brother and I love to play video games by _____ .
>   We don't like our sisters to play with us. (Jake M., San Antonio)
>
> - My husband likes to cook by _____ . And that's OK with
>   me! (Lidia S., Boston)
>
> - My daughter is very enthusiastic, and she likes to do extreme sports by
>   _____ . It makes me nervous! (Na-young K., San Francisco)
>
> What do you like to do by _____ ?

5 Complete the conversations with the correct personal and reflexive pronouns.

A. **Rachel:** _____I_____ like your scarf, Phoebe.
        ₁

   Phoebe: Thanks. I made it by _____ .
                                        ₂

   Rachel: Wow. _____ have a lot of talent!
                         ₃

B. **Sheila:** Look! My son painted this by _____ .
                                                ₁

   Feng: _____ did a great job.
                 ₂

C. **Joe:** Did you hear what happened to Emily?

   Martin: No, _____ didn't.
                       ₁

   Joe: She hurt _____ skiing.
                         ₂

   Martin: Is _____ OK?
                     ₃

   Joe: Yes, she is.

D. **Laura:** We really enjoyed _____ at your party, Pedro.
                                      ₁

   Pedro: I'm glad _____ had fun, but the food I made was terrible.
                           ₂

   Laura: Don't blame _____ . It was fine.
                               ₃

   Pedro: You're right. My friends enjoyed _____ . That's what counts!
                                                   ₄

6 Answer the questions with your own information.

Example: _Yes, I do. I'm very enthusiastic about good music._ or
           No, I don't. I'm not enthusiastic about anything.

1. Do you consider yourself enthusiastic? What are you enthusiastic about? _____

_____

2. Do you consider yourself flexible, or do you like to do things your own way? _____

_____

3. What do you like to do by yourself? _____

_____

4. Have you ever painted yourself? What did the picture look like? _____

_____

5. Do you know someone who hurt himself or herself playing a sport? What happened? _____

_____

6. Do you think people should travel by themselves? Why or why not? _____

_____

B I'll give it some thought.

1 Write the conversation in the correct order.

> Their prices are really high. You should go to Comp.com. It's an online store.
> ✓ Hi, Tina. Where are you going?
> Hmm. . . . I'll give it some thought. Thanks.
> I don't think you should do that.
> I'm going to Tech-It to buy a new computer.
> Really? Why not?

Erin: _Hi, Tina. Where are you going?_

Tina: _____

Erin: _____

Tina: _____

Erin: _____

Tina: _____

2 Complete the conversations. Use information from the pictures and sentences from the box. Use Exercise 1 as a model. Sometimes more than one answer is possible.

> I wouldn't recommend that.   I'll think about it.
> I'll see.   I'm not sure that's the best idea.

1. **Ed:** Hi, Ali. Where are you going?

   Ali: I'm going to _____ to

   buy a new _____ .

   Ed: _____ .

   Ali: Really? _____ ?

   Ed: Their prices are really high. You should go

   to _____ . It's an

   _____ store.

   Ali: Hmm. . . . _____ .
   Thanks.

2. **Sasha:** Hi, Marc. _____ ?

   Marc: I'm going to _____

   _____ .

   Sasha: _____ .

   Marc: Really? _____ ?

   Sasha: Their prices are really high.

   _____ .

   _____ .

   Marc: Hmm. . . . _____ .
   Thanks.

What would you do?

1 Rewrite the sentences. Change the underlined words. Use the phrasal verb in parentheses and the correct pronoun.

1. Can you <u>show me where Linda is</u>? (point out)

   Can you point her out?

2. You need to <u>do your homework again</u>. It has a lot of mistakes. (do over)

3. I <u>didn't accept that job</u>. (turn down)

4. I'm going to <u>donate these shirts</u>. (give away)

5. Please don't <u>mention his daughter</u>. (bring up)

6. When are you going to <u>return the money I lent you</u>? (pay back)

7. We really should <u>discuss our problem</u>. (talk over)

8. Can I <u>use this computer</u> before I buy it? (try out)

9. I'll <u>return your camera</u> tomorrow, if that's OK. (give back)

10. Let's <u>do the conference call later</u>. (put off)

2 Complete Bianca's email with the correct forms of the verbs in parentheses. Use the second conditional.

To: RobbieJ@cup.org
From: Bianca54@cup.com
Subject: What would you do?

Hi Rob,

I have some interesting news. My aunt might give me some money! I __*would do*__
                                                                              1
(do) so many things if I _____ (have) a lot of money. If I
                                      2
_____ (be) rich, I _____ (not work) anymore! That
           3   4
would be great. If I _____ (not have) a job, I _____
                              5   6
(travel) around the world. I _____ (feel) very lucky if I
                                         7
_____ (get) a lot of money. What would you do?
           8
Your friend,

Bianca

3 Now complete Rob's email with the correct forms of the verbs in parentheses. Use the second conditional.

To: Bianca54@cup.com
From: RobbieJ@cup.org
Subject: RE: What would you do?

Hey Bianca!

Wow! It __*would be*__ (be) great if your aunt _____ (give)
                  1   2
you money. Is it a lot of money? If I _____ (have) a lot of money, I
                                                3
_____ (make) a big, beautiful garden. But I can't have a garden at my
           4
apartment, so I _____ (need) a house with a big yard. I
                          5
_____ (use) a lot of my money to buy a house, and there
           6
_____ (be) a lot of room for two big gardens: a vegetable garden and a
           7
flower garden. I _____ (give) some money to my brother, too, if I
                          8
_____ (be) rich. He _____ (not have to pay) me back.
           9   10
Take care,

Rob

4 Write questions with the words in parentheses. Use the second conditional.

1. (What / you / do / if / you / be / braver)

   What would you do if you were braver?

2. (What / you / buy / for your friends / if / you / have / a lot of money)

   _____

3. (Where / you / go / if / you / have / a free ticket)

   _____

4. (What / you / do / if / you / have / 200 vacation days)

   _____

5. (What instrument / you / play / if / you and your friends / have / a band)

   _____

6. (What sport / you / try / if / you / try / an extreme sport)

   _____

7. (What / you / give away / if / you / move)

   _____

5 Answer the questions in Exercise 4 with your own information.

   Example: *If I were braver, I would take a trip around the world by myself.*

   1. _____
   2. _____
   3. _____
   4. _____
   5. _____
   6. _____
   7. _____

D What an accomplishment!

1 Read the letter. Then circle the correct answers.

1. How old is Thomas?   99   100   101

2. Who is Peter?   his brother   his son   his grandson

Dear Peter,

Can you believe I'll be 100 years old next week? If I had a dollar for every great thing I did, I would be rich! I decided to write to you about a few important things that happened in each decade of my life.

1920s – These are the first years I really remember. Jazz music was extremely popular, and I was in a jazz band. We were very dedicated to our music!

1930s – Many people didn't have a lot of money in the 1930s, but I worked very hard. In 1937, I bought myself a car! If I had that car today, it would be worth a lot of money!

1940s – This was a sad decade because of World War II, but the 1940s were also happy for me in many ways. I met your grandmother in 1941 when I was a soldier. A friend pointed her out to me at the supermarket. We got married two years later. That was a wise decision! Your mother was born in 1944.

1950s – We bought our first TV. I remember trying it out in the store first. It was amazing! And with the Civil Rights Movement starting, it was a good time to have a TV.

1960s – This was a very creative time in my life. Your grandmother was painting, and I started taking pictures. In 1969, a man walked on the moon!

1970s – I was offered a promotion in 1972, but I turned it down. I retired six years later.

1980s – I started a volunteer program at a hospital in 1982 and was busy with that for several years.

1990s – In 1995, a park in our town was dedicated to me for the volunteer work I did at the hospital. Do you remember when you bought me a computer in 1997? I never taught myself how to use it!

2000s – The 2000s were a quiet decade, but I've had a lot of time to spend with family. I bought a cell phone this year, but I took it back. I didn't think I really needed it. I guess I'm a little old-fashioned!

See you next week for my birthday!

Your grandfather,

Thomas O'Malley

2 Read the letter again. Then number the events in the correct order.

_____ He turned down a promotion.   _____ He got a cell phone.

_____ He got married.   _____ He bought a car.

_____ He started a volunteer program.   _____ He started taking pictures.

__1__ He was in a jazz band.   _____ He got a computer.

Music

 A *Music trivia*

1 Put the words in the correct order to make phrases about music. Add hyphens, if necessary.

1. best / artist / selling   *best-selling artist* _____

2. video / winning / award   _____

3. performer / often / downloaded   _____

4. priced / high / ticket   _____

5. group / named / oddly   _____

6. singers / well / known   _____

7. breaking / hit / record   _____

8. nice / voice / sounding   _____

2 Complete the webpage with the phrases from Exercise 1.

Jake and Jill's Music Awards

Hello fans! Here's today's music news from your favorite music fans!

- Sting, a _*best-selling artist*_ from the 1980s, and his wife started the
  1
  Rainforest Concert in 1991. They have the concert every two years. This year,

  _____ , like Elton John and Bruce Springsteen,
  2
  performed. Tickets were $2,500 or more! That's a _____ ,
  3
  but all of the money helps save rain forests around the world.

- Listen to *Yellow Fever!* It's a great album by Señor Coconut and His Orchestra. Yes, this

  is a very _____ (*señor* is a Spanish word, but Señor
  4
  Coconut is actually German), but we think each singer has a very

  _____ !
  5

- Who is the most _____ on our website? Taylor Swift!
  6
  Her song "Love Story" has been downloaded over 4 million times, and the video won the

  Country Music Association Award for Best Music Video in 2009. To listen to her

  _____ , *click here*. To watch her
  7

  _____ , *click here*.
  8

3 Complete the sentences with the correct forms of the words in parentheses. Use the past passive.

We Are the World

Kenny Rogers and Lionel Richie

"We Are the World" __was recorded__ (record) in 1985.
                          1
The money it made _____ (give) to groups
                               2
that help hungry people in Africa. The song

_____ (write) by Michael Jackson and Lionel
          3
Richie. Many famous singers, like Kenny Rogers, Bob Dylan, and

Stevie Wonder, _____ (ask) to sing it.
                          4

A video _____ (make) while the singers were recording the song. The song
                    5

and video _____ (play) on TV in the spring of 1985.
                    6

In 2010, "We Are the World" _____ (record) again with new singers to help
                                         7

the people of Haiti. The song _____ (sing) by over 80 well-known musicians,
                                        8

like Justin Bieber and Jennifer Hudson. It _____ (see) on TV by many people
                                                        9

on February 12.

4 Rewrite each sentence in the past passive. If there is information about who did the action, use a *by* phrase.

1. Four men planned the Woodstock Festival in 1969.

   The Woodstock Festival was planned by four men in 1969.

2. Someone asked many well-known singers to sing at Woodstock.

   _____

3. Someone gave information about the festival on the radio.

   _____

4. Someone allowed about 400,000 to 500,000 music fans into the festival.

   _____

5. People made a documentary about Woodstock in 1970.

   _____

6. *Rolling Stone* magazine listed Woodstock as one of "50 Moments that Changed the History of Rock and Roll."

   _____

5 Look at the chart of some record-breaking hits. Then answer the questions. Use the past passive.

Song	Singer(s)	Year of release	Millions of recordings sold
Candle in the Wind	Elton John	1997	37
White Christmas	Bing Crosby	1942	30
We Are the World	Many musicians	1985	20
Rock Around the Clock	Bill Haley and his Comets	1954	17
I Want to Hold Your Hand	The Beatles	1963	12
Hey Jude	The Beatles	1968	10
It's Now or Never	Elvis Presley	1960	10
I Will Always Love You	Whitney Houston	1992	10

1. Who was "It's Now or Never" sung by?   *It was sung by Elvis Presley.*

2. When was "White Christmas" released?   _____

3. Who were "I Want to Hold Your Hand" and "Hey Jude" sung by?   _____

4. How many recordings of "We Are the World" were sold?   _____

5. What song was released in 1954?   _____

6. What song was sung by Elton John?   _____

7. How many recordings of "I Will Always Love You" were sold?   _____

8. When was "Hey Jude" released?   _____

6 Answer the questions with your own information. Write complete sentences.

Example: *My favorite song was "Candle in the Wind."*

1. What was your favorite song when you were 12?   _____

2. Who was it sung by?   _____

3. What kind of music was it?   _____

4. Was a video made of the song? What was it like?   _____

5. Was the singer or group well known?   _____

6. Is the singer or group well known today?   _____

7. Did you ever go to a concert of the singer or group? Where was it?   _____

8. Was a documentary ever made about the singer or group? What was it called?   _____

B The first thing you do is . . .

Rewrite the instructions. Use the words in the box.

A.

> **How to Buy a Song**
> 1. Find the song you want, and click on it.
> 2. Enter your credit card number.
> 3. Read the information, and click "Yes."

| After that | ✓First | To finish |

How to Buy a Song

First, find the song you want, and click on it. _____

_____

_____

B.

> **How to Listen to Music on Your Phone**
> 1. Open your music program.
> 2. Choose the song you want to listen to.
> 3. Click "Play."

| The last thing you do is | Then | To start |

How to Listen to Music on Your Phone

_____

_____

_____

C.

> **How to Record Your Voice**
> 1. Put the recorder near you.
> 2. Hit the "Record" button.
> 3. Sing a song or speak into the recorder.

| Finally | Next | The first thing you do is |

How to Record Your Voice

_____

_____

_____

C Music and me

1 Complete the sentences and the puzzle with the correct verbs.

Across

1. My favorite band will _____ a new album next week.

5. Justin Bieber sang the song "My World," but he didn't _____ it.
Usher was one of the producers.

7. Coldplay will _____ their tour dates on their website.

8. Beethoven couldn't hear anything, but he was able to _____ great music.
Many people listen to his music today, almost 200 years after he died.

Down

2. Lady Gaga likes to _____ her audience in her concerts.

3. I can't sing very well, but I really _____ music. I listen to it all the time.

4. Do you know when your brother's band is going to _____ their new song?
I really would like to go see his band.

6. We're going to _____ our new song in the studio next week.
They have new computers we can use.

2 Circle the correct word to complete each sentence.

1. Beethoven's Fifth Symphony is my favorite musical **compose** / (**composition**).

2. My favorite band **released** / **a release** a new album yesterday.

3. My uncle **produces** / **production** songs, but he can't sing or play an instrument.

4. Jonathan found one of his father's old **record** / **recordings**.

5. Wendy loves to go to **perform** / **performances** at music festivals.

6. My sister likes to **entertain** / **entertainment** our family.

7. The band made an **announce** / **announcement** about their tour yesterday.

8. What time does the **produce** / **production** of *Hamlet* start?

3 Answer the questions with your own information. Write complete sentences.

Example: <u>*My favorite kind of entertainment is the movies.*</u>

1. What's your favorite kind of entertainment? _____

2. Have you ever taken a music class? When? _____

3. Have you ever heard your favorite singer perform? Where? _____

4. Have you ever been to a party for an album release? Where? _____

5. What kind of music do you appreciate? _____

4 Complete the email with *yet* or *already*.

To: Lee1988@cup.org
From: JJJ@cup.com
Subject: Do you have plans on Friday night?

Hey Lee!

Have you made plans for Friday night _____*yet*_____ ? My brother's band,
                                                    1
Time Travel, is playing at the Music Café. I've _____ seen them
                                                                          2
about ten times, and they're great! Have you listened to the CD I sent you

_____ ? I've _____ bought tickets for my sister
            3   4
and me, but I haven't gotten a ticket for you _____ . Let me know
                                                                  5
if you want to go. Tickets aren't high-priced. They're only $10. Time Travel has

_____ started recording their next CD. It hasn't been released
            6
_____ , but they might play a few songs from it on Friday. I hope
            7
you can come!

Jay

5 Look at Carla's To-Do list. Then write sentences about what she has and hasn't done. Use the present perfect with *yet* or *already*.

> *To Do*
> Send Jen and Sandra information about the Coldplay concert ✔
> Call Sandra and Jen about tickets to see Coldplay ✔
> Buy the tickets ✔
> Clean the house
> Go to the airport to pick up Jen and Sandra

1. *Carla has already sent Jen and Sandra information about the Coldplay concert.*
2. *She* _____
3. _____
4. _____
5. _____

6 Look at Jen and Sandra's To-Do list. Then write questions and answers about what they have and haven't done. Use the present perfect with *yet* or *already*.

> *To Do*
> Do the laundry ✔
> Clean the apartment ✔
> Listen to Coldplay's new songs
> Give our parents Carla's cell phone number ✔
> Pay Carla for the tickets

1. Question: *Have Jen and Sandra done the laundry yet?*

   Answer: *Yes, they have already done the laundry.*

2. Q: *Have they* _____

   A: _____

3. Q: _____

   A: _____

4. Q: _____

   A: _____

5. Q: _____

   A: _____

D Thoughts on music

1 Read the article. Then write why musicians don't want people to give music to their friends.

_____

Music Laws

Today, many people get their music from the Internet. But is it legal? It depends on how you get the music and what country you live in. It's sometimes OK, but it's often against the law.

It is usually legal to buy songs from websites on the Internet. If you buy a song, you can make a copy for yourself. However, in the United States and some other countries, it is illegal to make copies of the song for your friends. This is because laws protect people's ideas and work. If everyone copied and gave music to their friends, people would not buy the singers' albums, and musicians couldn't make money for their work.

Also, in many countries it's illegal to *bootleg* music. This is a word that describes when people go to a live performance, record the music, and then upload the music to the Internet to give to their friends or to sell. Sometimes at concerts musicians perform new songs before they are recorded in a studio. They don't want their music released on the Internet before their albums are sold.

Some people *sample* music when they compose songs. This means they use a part of someone else's song in their music. This is often done in hip-hop music. Sampling is usually legal if you have permission from the singer, but it is usually not OK to use someone else's music without permission.

Interesting Music Trivia

- In 1990, part of a David Bowie song was sampled by Vanilla Ice without permission. After the song was released, Vanilla Ice had to pay David Bowie a lot of money for using his music.

- In 1999, Napster was created as a way to get music from friends without paying for it on the Internet. Napster had to stop doing this in the United States, and now people have to pay for the music.

2 Read the article. Then write L (legal – OK) or I (illegal – not OK) for these actions according to the laws in the United States.

1. You can buy songs on the Internet from websites. ___*L*___

2. You can get a song for free from a friend. _____

3. You can bootleg music from a live performance. _____

4. You can sample music without permission. _____

On vacation

A Travel preferences

1 Complete the travel ads with the correct phrases from the box.

buy handicrafts	listen to live music	✓speak a foreign language	visit landmarks
go to clubs	see wildlife	try local food	volunteer

European Vacation

Can you __speak a__
__foreign language__ ₁?
If you speak French,
Spanish, or Portuguese, this
is the vacation for you! Visit
France, Spain, and Portugal.
_____ ₂,
like the Eiffel Tower in France and famous
museums in Spain, or stay near the ocean
in Portugal.

Miami Dream

The weather is wonderful in
Miami for most of the year.
Visit beaches during the day.
At night,
_____ ₅
to dance! There are also
many places to
_____ ₆.
You can go to a concert or listen to free music
in the parks or even on the beach.

South American Working Vacation

Visit Peru and Ecuador in a different way.
_____ your time to ₃
help people and animals. First, teach English
in Peru, and then work in the Amazon rain
forest. You'll _____ ₄,
like frogs, river dolphins, and monkeys.

Seoul Markets

Do you like shopping? Tour Seoul's markets.
Namdaemun is the largest market in Seoul, and
it sells many different things. You can
_____ , like bags and ₇
jewelry. You can even _____ ₈
while you are shopping at the market or take
some home to cook.

2 Put the words in the correct order to make sentences. Make one of the words a gerund. Use the simple present forms of the other verbs.

1. be / by boat / Travel / very slow

   Traveling by boat is very slow.

2. enjoy / I / foreign languages / speak / when I travel

   _____

3. buy / handicrafts for my cousins / I / in local markets / like

   _____

4. be / to cook / I / interested in / learn / Thai food

   _____

5. be / to do on vacation / landmarks / my favorite thing / Visit

   _____

6. be / concerned about / help / I / wildlife in the ocean

   _____

3 Complete the conversation with the gerund forms of the correct words from the box.

| go   ✓hike   travel   volunteer   volunteer |

Mark: Hey, Jesse. Where are you going for vacation?

Jesse: I don't know. I enjoy _____*hiking*_____ in
        ₁
        the mountains. Any suggestions?

Mark: How about the Rockies in Canada?

Jesse: I don't think so. I prefer _____
        ₂
        somewhere warm.

Mark: Why don't you go to Costa Rica? There are
        mountains there, and it's warm.

Jesse: That's a good idea. You know, I'm interested in _____ .
        ₃
        Maybe I could help animals there.

Mark: _____ is a great idea. It should make the vacation cheaper,
        ₄
        too. Are you going by yourself?

Jesse: No, I'm not. I dislike _____ alone. I'm going with friends.
        ₅

4 Look at the chart. Then complete the sentences.

Name	Travel activity	Opinion	Preference
Cara	travel / by bus	slow	go / by train
Diego	drive / a car	dangerous	ride / a bike
Donna and Nicole	visit / landmarks	boring	see / wildlife
Tom	go / to clubs	not fun	go / to concerts
Ian and Meg	travel / by plane	expensive	stay / home
Libby	learn / Chinese	difficult	study / Spanish

1. Cara thinks _traveling by bus is slow_ . She prefers _going by train_ .

2. Diego thinks _____ . He _____ .

3. Donna and Nicole think _____ . They _____ .

4. Tom thinks _____ . He _____ .

5. Ian and Meg _____ . They _____ .

6. Libby _____ . She _____ .

5 Answer the questions with your own information. Use gerunds when possible.

Example: _I'm interested in buying handicrafts and trying local food._

1. What vacation activities are you interested in? _____

2. What do you enjoy doing on vacation? _____

3. What do you dislike doing on vacation? _____

4. What do you think is the easiest way to travel? _____

5. What do you think is the cheapest way to travel? _____

6. What do you dislike about planning a vacation? _____

7. What are you concerned about when looking for a hotel? _____

_____

8. What do you worry about when you travel? _____

9. Do you like listening to live local music when you travel? What kind? _____

_____

10. Are you interested in writing about your vacations? Why or why not? _____

_____

Don't forget to . . .

Complete the conversations with sentences from the box.

> Don't forget to get to the station 20 minutes early.
> Let me remind you to get there before 8:00 p.m.
> Remember to look for plane tickets today.
> ✓Would you like a bus ticket or a train ticket?
> Would you prefer one bed or two beds?
> Would you rather go to a warm place or a cold place?

A. Mr. Harris: Hello. Can I help you?

Richard: Yes. I'd like a ticket for Chicago, please.

Mr. Harris: OK. <u>*Would you like a bus ticket*</u>
₁
<u>*or a train ticket*</u> ?
₁

Richard: Oh, well, which one is better?

Mr. Harris: The bus takes longer, but it's cheaper.

Richard: Hmm. . . . I'll take the bus. I'm going on Saturday morning.

Mr. Harris: Good. A bus leaves at 9:15. _____ .
₂

Richard: OK. Thanks.

B.   Blanca: Hey, Erica. _____ .
₁

Erica: Oh, yeah. Thanks. I'll look for the best tickets online after work.

_____ ?
₂

Blanca: Let's go somewhere hot, like the beach.

Erica: OK. I'll look for some cheap tickets, and we can make plans tonight.

Blanca: Great. Thanks.

C.   Ms. Ito: Can I help you?

Shan: Yes, I need a room for three nights.

Ms. Ito: No problem. _____ ?
₁

Shan: One bed, please. Oh, and is there a restaurant in this hotel?

Ms. Ito: Yes, there is. It's right over there. _____ .
₂
It closes at 8:30.

Rules and recommendations

1 Complete the words for the extreme sports.

1. p*aragliding*_____

2. r_____
   c_____

3. b_____
   j_____

4. w_____ -
   w_____
   r_____

5. k_____
   s_____

6. w_____

7. s_____

8. s_____

2 Circle the correct expression to complete each sentence.

1. **Necessity:** _____ fill out this form before you go paragliding.

   a. You don't have to   (b.) You must   c. You'd better

2. **Recommendation:** Sandra _____ plan her vacation before she goes.

   a. doesn't have to   b. must   c. ought to

3. **Lack of necessity:** You _____ wear warm clothes when rock climbing in the summer.

   a. don't have to   b. have to   c. shouldn't

4. **Necessity:** Nancy and Carol _____ wear heavy boots when they go snowboarding.

   a. should   b. shouldn't   c. have to

5. **Recommendation:** _____ take sunglasses when you go white-water rafting.

   a. You must   b. You've got to   c. You'd better

6. **Lack of necessity:** Jorge _____ go skydiving if he doesn't want to.

   a. has to   b. doesn't have to   c. shouldn't

7. **Necessity:** _____ pay for my kite surfing lessons before I can take the first lesson.

   a. I've got to   b. I don't have to   c. I'd better

8. **Recommendation:** Sue and Teddy _____ go bungee jumping. It's very dangerous.

   a. don't have to   b. have got to   c. shouldn't

3 Complete the article with *must* or *should*.

✈ *How to Get to Your Flight Faster*

Airports have a lot of rules. Here are some tips to help you get through the airport faster.

Airport Security

- You _____should_____ print your boarding pass at home,
  1
  if possible.

- You _____ get to the airport early. It's a good
  2
  idea to arrive an hour before your flight.

- You _____ have your passport or other ID.
  3
  You can't get on the plane without one of them.

- You _____ take off your shoes at security.
  4
  They won't let you go through with them on.

- You _____ wear shoes that are easy to take off.
  5
  You'll move faster.

4 Circle the correct words to complete the instructions.

Welcome to the Riverside Park white-water rafting trip. We want you to have a safe trip, so there are a few things that you **(have to)** / **don't have to** do.
1

First of all, **you'd better** / **you shouldn't** listen to your guide. That's me, so please
2
listen to me carefully. Now for the safety rules: **You must not** / **You must** sit on the
3
raft at all times. Stand only when you are getting on or off the raft. And while we are riding, you **don't have to** / **ought to** hold on to the raft.
4

It's going to be warm today, so you **don't have to** / **must** wear a coat, but you
5
should / **shouldn't** wear a hat. It will protect your skin and eyes from the sun. Later
6
we'll stop at a beach and have lunch there. **You shouldn't** / **You'd better** eat on the raft.
7
Finally, don't forget that rafting can be dangerous. **You don't have to** / **You've got to**
8
be careful all day. If you follow my instructions, you'll be safe and have fun!

5 Write your own rules and recommendations for each place. Use modals for necessity, lack of necessity, and recommendations.

Example: **In a restaurant:** 1. <u>*You must pay for your food.*</u>

2. <u>*You don't have to eat something you don't like.*</u>

3. <u>*You should leave a little extra money for the waiter or waitress.*</u>

In a restaurant:

1. _____

2. _____

3. _____

At the movies:

4. _____

5. _____

6. _____

In your classroom:

7. _____

8. _____

9. _____

1 Read the catalogue page. Then number the pictures to match the descriptions.

World Tour The Catalogue for Travelers

Every year, World Tour chooses the top five items every traveler must have. Read about what you should buy this year.

1. Digi-2300 Camera $129.99

Every traveler ought to have a good, reliable digital camera. We recommend the Digi-2300. It's small, so you can easily take it anywhere. It's great for taking pictures of landmarks or just for taking pictures of your friends. It's a reasonable price, and it takes great pictures.

2. XP Binoculars $52.99

Look through these fantastic binoculars to see wildlife on your next safari. Using them is a great way to see animals safely and up close. They make the animals look ten times larger. You can also use these binoculars underwater, so they're great for looking at fish, too. They will fit easily in your bag because they're very small. Put them in your bag next to your new camera!

To order, call (800) 555-3400 or visit our website at www.worldtour.com/cup

3. Simple Sarong $18.50

Sarongs are very useful, and there's one size for everyone. Women can use sarongs as a skirt or a dress, but men can use them, too. They work well as towels for the beach or to use after swimming, waterskiing, and kite surfing. Dry your body off, and then the towel dries in minutes! Get it in blue, black, red, orange, or green.

4. Earplugs   2 for $3.50

Earplugs are a cheap and practical gift for a friend or for yourself. Traveling on airplanes, buses, and trains can be noisy, but you won't hear any noise with these earplugs. Put them in your ears and fall asleep!

5. The "It Bag" $75.00

Our best bag is called the "It Bag" because you have to have it! It can be small or large because it's expandable. It's perfect for a day trip or for a weekend vacation. Get it in black, brown, or red.

2 Read the catalogue page again. Then write T (true), F (false), or NI (no information).

1. The binoculars are cheaper than the camera. __T__

2. The camera only comes in one color. _____

3. You have to wear the sarong. _____

4. The earplugs aren't expensive. _____

5. Expanding the bag is easy. _____

Credits

Illustration credits

Kveta Jelinek: 62, 73; Andrew Joyner: 50; Greg Paprocki: 55, 70, 77; Garry Parsons: 49, 71; Maria Rabinky: 93; Rob Schuster: 76; Richard Williams: 68, 75

Photography credits

51 ©Mike Powell/Getty Images; 52 (top to bottom) ©Iain Masterton/Alamy; ©Rene Magritte/Bridgeman Art Library/Superstock; ©Charles Stirling/Alamy; ©Oleksiy Maksymenko/Alamy; 57 (clockwise from top left) ©Media Bakery; ©Marlene Ford/Alamy; ©Franz Aberham/Getty Images; 60 ©Alamy; 61 (clockwise from top left) ©Justin Prenton/Alamy; ©Photo Library; ©Media Bakery; ©Media Bakery; ©Photo Library; ©Media Bakery; 63 (top to bottom) ©Fuse/Getty Images; ©Media Bakery; ©Fancy/Alamy; ©Media Bakery; ©Media Bakery; ©Media Bakery; 64 ©Media Bakery; 69 ©Media Bakery; 74 ©Tomás del Amo/Alamy; 79 (left to right) ©Ian Miles – Flashpoint Pictures/Alamy; ©Magdalena Rehova/Alamy; ©Media Bakery; (bottom) ©Tyler Stableford/Getty Images; 82 ©Redferns/Getty Images; 84 ©Frederick Bass/Getty Images; 87 ©Jason LaVeris/Getty Images; 89 (clockwise from top left) ©Jay Reilly/Getty Images; ©Media Bakery; ©Wendy Connett/Alamy; ©Alamy; 90 ©Nicolas Russell/Getty Images; 92 ©Photo Edit; 94 ©Alamy; 96 (left to right) ©Shutterstock; ©Shutterstock; ©Theo Fitzhugh/Alamy; ©Creative Crop/Getty Images; ©Creative Crop/Getty Images